D1592786

INTIMACY AND RITUAL

A Study of Spiritualism,
Mediums and Groups

INTIMACY AND RITUAL
A Study of Spiritualism,
Mediums and Groups

VIEDA SKULTANS

Routledge & Kegan Paul
London and Boston

First published in 1974
by Routledge & Kegan Paul Ltd
Broadway House, 68–74 *Carter Lane,*
London EC4V 5EL and
9 *Park Street,*
Boston, Mass. 02108, *U.S.A.*
Printed in Great Britain by
John Sherratt and Son Limited, Park Road,
Timperley, Altrincham, Cheshire WA14 5QQ
© *Vieda Skultans* 1974
No part of this book may be reproduced in
any form without permission from the
publisher, except for the quotation of brief
passages in criticism

ISBN 0 7100 7760 2
Library of Congress Catalog Card No. 73-87318

Contents

Preface

Spiritualism is no longer associated with materialization; the production of this book is, therefore, a reversion to that former era only in the sense that this book is a material offering arising from spiritualist activities. I sincerely thank all those spiritualists whose private sorrows and religious learning are the subject-matter of this book. Their generous response to inquiry made field-work both intellectually and emotionally rewarding. I have written this book not as a religious treatise but from the standpoint of an observer interested in social relationships. Hence, the focus of interest of the book is different from that of a spiritualist. I hope, however, that no offence is taken for anything written herein—as none is certainly intended.

I also wish to thank Dr Joe Loudon who, as my Ph.D. supervisor, listened patiently to the vicissitudes of my field-work career.

Finally, I am indebted to the Department of Health and Social Security who financed the research, the more so since the outcome of the research does not match their expectations.

This book is based on field-work carried out over a period of three years in South Wales. Being trained as a social anthropologist I became a 'participant observer' among spiritualists in a town which I call Welshtown. This involved attending spiritualist services and meetings as well as talking to spiritualists in their own homes and on the way to services. As a non-religious observer my aims were to provide as complete a description as possible of spiritualist activities and to relate these to the secular portion of their lives. Within this general aim is included the more specifically theological one of giving an accurate account of spiritualist doctrine and beliefs about the spirit world. As a participant I tried to understand at a more subjective level the rewards which spiritualism offers to its believers.

It is difficult to obtain an accurate figure of the total spiritualist population in Welshtown, because there is no formal acknowledgment of membership of a spiritualist church. I estimate that there are about four hundred, most of whom are working class. About three hundred are women, generally middle-aged and older. My general impression is that spiritualists are not newcomers to Welshtown but come from families long-established in South Wales.

I attended up to five meetings a week during the peak of my enthusiasm, but I never found this to be a chore. From the outset I made a point of explaining my role as researcher and observer. However, my research aims proved in no way to be an embarrassment or hindrance since all spiritualists consider themselves to be engaged in research in some measure. Thus my interest, as interpreted by spiritualists, did not make me significantly different from others, since all spiritualists consider that they are researching into the spirit world. Indeed, my initial self-conscious declaration of intent was soon forgotten and never referred to again.

Field-work was made enjoyable by the warm and un-questioning acceptance which I was given. Furthermore, I found myself readily able to identify with spiritualists. Their preoccupation with the privacy of pain, their experience of isolation and their anxieties about communication are in-tellectually interesting and emotionally intelligible. I do not look upon them as 'seedy solipsists' to use Samuel Beckett's phrase describing the depressed Schubert. However, although their disaster-expectant outlook did not disturb me, I cannot accept their solutions or rejoice in their spiritual rewards. In this respect neither participation nor identification was com-plete, by which I mean that I am not myself a spiritualist. Al-though their sorrows did not depress me, their joys did.

The welcome and ready acceptance which I received was particularly strong in the developing circle, where I did most of my research. This circle meets weekly in a spiritualist church in the industrial outskirts of Welshtown. I gained entry to this circle through one of the members of a WEA class which I gave. This woman was a member of my class and also a long-established member of the circle. Through her I was introduced to the leader of the circle and subsequently granted full membership. Much of what I know about spiritualism was learnt from members of the circle, which is referred to through-out the book.

The 'home' or 'developing' circle is the most widespread and important form of spiritualist encounter. Both terms are literally descriptive. The former term refers to the group's setting; the latter to its functions. Circles are run by mediums of long-standing and high reputation. The circle meets regularly, often in the home of the medium. Its aims are to develop the latent and nascent mediumistic powers of its members and thus to produce fully-fledged mediums. In view of its intimate setting the circle can be seen as a private rehearsal for the grand début which takes place at a spiritualist service. This form of organization is a reflection of spiritualist ideology which has as one of its basic tenets the belief that everyone possesses psychic power in a latent if not fully developed form. (This belief is, of course, consistent with the fact that most people never develop their mediumistic potential at all.) Entrance to such circles is difficult to obtain. Frequently this is achieved by making one's psychic gifts known publicly and especially to well-established mediums associated with the coveted circle. Continued and regular attendance is, it is thought, essential if good results are to be obtained. Developing circles should never be large and the optimum number is thought to be about twelve. One of the underlying premises of developing circles is that progress in mediumistic performance achieved by one member affects every other member of the group in a positive way.

Although there is a written tradition of thought about spiritualism and official doctrine is available at any one of the spiritualist headquarters, its influence at the local level is insignificant. Practice and belief seem to be determined by local needs and inspiration rather than by documentation from a central authority. This is explained in part by an explicit emphasis on individual inspiration and in part by an inherent weakness in organizational and co-ordinating abilities. This lack of influence of official doctrine is apparent in that few spiritualists are aware of which national organization, if any, their church belongs to; let alone do they know the doctrinal differences consequent upon such membership.

Religious beliefs and practices are learnt from other more developed mediums, usually in the context of the developing circle. In fact, there is a stigma attached to learning about spiritualism, especially mediumship and healing, from published material. The true path to spiritual power, as, indeed, to much therapeutic art, is through regular contact with, and encouragement from, a small number of more advanced adepts.

Spiritualist women in Welshtown are frequently the daughters of spiritualist mediums. Thus first introduction to the movement takes place in childhood but a regular link is not established until later on in adulthood, usually after marriage.

Throughout this book spiritualism is seen in terms of the coping techniques and the rewards which it is able to offer its members. It therefore provides one example of Gerald Caplan's notion of an 'informal support system' (1972) but such a description of spiritualism is incomplete without reference to other support systems which Welshtown is able to offer. The question to be borne in mind is: 'What are the alternatives available to the traditionally feminine woman who is trying to cope with problems arising from or related to her role?' By traditional feminine role I mean one whose activities are confined to being a housewife, mother and sexual partner, or, where this is not possible, as in the case of a spinster or barren married woman, where she nevertheless tries to approximate to this role.

It is not necessary to supply an exhaustive summary of the care-giving organizations in South Wales. Suffice it to say that formal organizations such as the psychiatric hospital and social work agencies are rarely considered as sources of problem-solving techniques, since, almost by definition, they imply total inadequacy and failure. Work, especially for the middle-aged, untrained woman who has spent a major part of her adult life rearing children and keeping house, is impossible to find. Furthermore, the cultural climate of South Wales is such that alternatives to the traditional feminine role do not receive the sanction of public approval. Work outside the home is seen as a means of augmenting the housekeeping money but rarely as an end in its own right creating new goals or as refurbishing an uncertain sense of self. Thus emotional problems are worked out within the confines imposed by the traditional feminine role. Indeed, this is where the contribution of spiritualism lies. For the weekly repetition of healing activities and the exchange of messages 'from spirit' constitute a ritual of reconciliation to a situation which does not permit any radical alternatives to itself. For more than half the women spiritualism had involved no 'shopping around' since their mothers had been spiritualists and had transmitted their interest to their daughters. For others, spiritualism had been arrived at after a long spiritual journey during which a number of different religious styles had been sampled, none of which had proved satisfactory. Only spiritualism had been found to give that quality of spiritual balm needed to make life palatable.

One of the problems which this book raises is that of cross-cultural comparison and definition. This problem has been referred to by Ioan Lewis (1966, p. 326) as that of trying to 'classify and hold constant a range of similar symptoms which are dealt with in a wide diversity of institutionalized ways in different societies'. The lowest common denominator problem is one of establishing whether spirit possession has a core of critical characteristics, on the basis of which one can compare, for example, spirit possession cults in South Wales with spirit possession cults in Africa.

My assumption is that a cross-cultural definition of spirit possession can be supplied and that this consists of two key elements. Spirit possession always relates to illness: possession involves a degree of mental or physical incapacity. This incapacity can vary either according to the severity of the illness or according to its duration. The range of the severity of the illness varies from complete insanity at one end of the scale to mild physical disabilities, such as headaches and muscular pains, at the other. The duration of the illness may also vary widely. In rare cases the incapacity may be of long duration. More frequently, however, incapacity takes the form of temporarily felt or shared symptoms of the possessing spirit. Nevertheless, in all cases of spirit possession, a link of varying degrees of strength and duration exists between the possessed person and illness. The second element in spirit possession is the assumption of roles which in the ordinary way lie beyond the social repertoire of the possessed person, but whose assumption during possession is mystically sanctioned. Thus in Welsh-town, spirit possession seances constitute a rehearsal of a wide-ranging number of roles by women who are otherwise only familiar with one role. For this reason it may be significant that developing circles are, in fact, circular in physical form. The circle encloses a central arena, a stage upon which the action or rehearsal can take place.

The dramatic and even theatrical aspects of spirit possession have frequently been remarked upon, but the full significance of this characterization, especially in its relation to illness, has not always been appreciated. The assumption of ordinarily inaccessible roles is not easy and even where such assumption is mystically sanctioned it is accompanied by illness. It may well be that women participants interpret spiritualist rehearsals as violating social boundaries and illness as the penalty which one pays for such transgression.

From the observer's point of view, however, illness facilitates the assumption of other roles by removing responsibility and accountability from the individual. Sociologists see the 'sick role' as characterized by the exemption from normal social responsibilities (see Parsons, 1950, p. 436). Possession illness is positively sought out and its successful cultivation is seen as art. There is no obligation to get well; indeed, there is a positive injunction to cultivate illness. This is because illness creates a vacuum as far as the norms defining one's customary obligations and responsibilities are concerned. It provides a niche into which new social roles can be introduced and in which they can be fostered.

A question frequently raised about spiritualism relates to the authenticity and sincerity of possession states. What proportion of such states are simulated? Regarding the genuine cases—what are the psychological requirements which facilitate trance and possession? Both questions are misplaced, for they ignore the social context in which possession occurs. How bodily sensations are identified and interpreted, and the importance which is attached to them will depend not upon the experiencing self or upon the intrinsic nature of the sensation, but upon the social interest expressed in particular sensations. Thus spiritualists are instructed not to 'sit' alone, but in circles under the guidance and leadership of an advanced medium. Sittings take place in semi-darkness so that members are not distracted by outward things but can direct their attention inwards. Instruction in mediumship involves attention to posture and breathing, as well as to the contents of the mind. When a state of suitable physical relaxation and mental calm has been achieved members are taught how to identify certain signs as indicative of possession. For example, sensations of heat or cold, tingling or throbbing may be interpreted as signs of the onset of possession. Thus possession does not require any prior peculiar state of mind but rather, membership of a social group in which detailed attention is given to bodily states and in which heightened awareness of such states allows them to be identified and defined in a special way. The spiritualist situation is remarkably similar to marijuana-smoking groups described by Jock Young (1971). Here, too, novices are urged not to smoke alone but in groups of more experienced smokers. Similarly, the bodily experiences induced by marijuana-smoking are thought to require interpretation and to be fully appreciated only if first identified for the novice by his more experienced colleagues.

If any extrinsic justification is needed to show the relevance of spiritualism to the mainstream of religious belief and practice then I would appeal to the widespread, if formally unacknow-ledged, belief in the spirit world and the possibility of communi-cation with it. This is frequently expressed in such phrases as: 'I don't believe in meddling in it,' or 'I think it's best left alone.' Such references to the dangers of communication with the spirit world also imply a tacit acknowledgment of its existence. However, not only do beliefs about the spirit world and mediumship exist at a general and implicit level, they are formally expressed within orthodox Christian thought. The publication of the Bishop of Exeter's report on *Exorcism* (1972) indicates the central importance which spiritualist concepts occupy within both the Anglican and the Roman Catholic churches. Thus the widespread nature of spiritualist beliefs should counter the notion that they are in any way marginal or the exclusive interest of an extremist sect.

The sequence of presentation of the book follows the course of field-work and the development of my thoughts on the subject. Chapter 2 is an account of some of the earlier services attended together with a description of some spiritualist mediums. Chapter 3 gives an account of spiritualist beliefs and practices with special emphasis on the concern with illness both as this reflects epistemological preoccupations and as the physical counterpart of social malaise. Chapter 4 describes healing activities and sees them as rituals of reconciliation involving ideal representations of male and female roles and marital harmony. Chapter 5 describes the conflict between mediums and churches resulting from the competition for scarce spiritual rewards. Chapter 6 examines the way in which spiritualist messages offer relevant symbols and explanations of illness and misfortune, thereby providing conceptual tools for ordering experience. Chapter 7 examines alternative explanations and coping techniques. Similarities between religious and therapeutic groups are offered.

Finally, it needs to be stressed that my field-work was limited to the churches and circles in Welshtown and that the conclusions drawn do not aim to be representative of spiritualist belief and practice as such. No doubt some features of spiritualist meetings in Welshtown will be totally absent in south-east England and vice versa. Fictional names have been given to all places, churches and individuals.

Chapter 2   The actors

The nature of the movement in South Wales can be readily conveyed by describing a number of church services. These services were attended at the beginning of my period of field-work. They therefore convey my impressions of spiritualist activities in a form which is relatively uninfluenced by theoretical assumptions. The accounts of church services are followed by a description of three leading local mediums. Before the descriptions of services and mediums, however, an outline of the two churches needs to be sketched.

I have named the first church 'Park Street' and the second 'King Street'. Park Street is very much a reception centre for new spiritualists. Significantly, messages are concerned with personal ailments and misfortunes. Of the two churches only Park Street provides a separate healing session once a week. For the present it is sufficient to note that pain and misfortune are the idiom in which an interest in spiritualism is first expressed. Messages tend to refer to physical disorders with little or no attempt at a deeper or more general understanding. The symbols appearing in messages are correspondingly trite, such as a bunch of flowers. However, judging by the numbers of new faces which continue to appear in Park Street, interest seldom continues to express itself solely as a preoccupation with bodily illness. The alternative provided by King Street is a staunch anti-male attitude, one which could be characterized as a 'withdrawal from traditional feminine roles' (Horton, 1969). King Street meetings follow a repetitive pattern, especially on Thursday afternoons. The meetings are

9

taken by old Mrs Davies, a former member of the developing circle. These meetings are not concerned with physical ailments, although most members are old and ill. Possibly the nature and tone of meetings are influenced by the fact that attendance is exclusively female. Mrs Davies's messages all refer to situations in which a harsh independent attitude is essential. She is repetitive, with a limited and well-worn vocabulary. For this reason it is difficult to remember the exact content of services. She says: 'Don't give an inch!' 'Don't give no satisfaction!' 'Be stubborn! Be obstinate! Be yourself, no matter what others say!' 'Be free!' 'Be independent!' 'You'll be up and they'll be down!' 'Be secretive! Watch all, but say nothing! You'll be laughing!' For the most part such messages seem to be easily understood by the women to whom they are addressed.

Further alternatives to King Street and Park Street are provided by developing circles. Their small size encourages intimacy which in turn permits a detailed exploration of the problems of its members. Such exploration is not possible in the larger groups and simpler tactics are suggested as ways of dealing with problem situations.

The following descriptions of services and mediums were written in the course of field-work:

First service in Park Street (March 1969)

I sat at the back in a row of middle-aged women. There were about thirty-five present, mostly women. Three women on my right were discussing the case of a relative, who was seriously ill in hospital.

The service was presided over by Mr Dear in the absence of Mrs Daimler. The sermon was read by a Mrs Scott from Llandare. She was a woman of about fifty with a forceful voice and manner. Her sermon was short. It concerned the way in which the spirit world impinged on and imbued the earth world. She referred to 'this little edifice' as a 'home from home'. Mrs Scott was very domineering when giving the addresses from the spirit world, especially if she received a half-hearted or ambiguous response from the person addressed.

Seven people were addressed altogether. This seems to be a typical number for one evening. It means that an average address or message lasts for about seven minutes.

A woman, who at a previous meeting had been told not to wash windows, was addressed first. This time her ailments were located in the region of the midriff. At this point my neighbour nudged me and said, 'She's right you know.' The woman addressed was told to take it easy for the next six months. She was told that she was well-endowed and that one day she would be taking Mrs Scott's place.

The next person addressed was a slightly overweight woman sitting next to me. She was told that her husband was in hospital with stomach trouble. It was affecting the glands in his throat. He should turn to the people of the spirit world if he wanted to be saved. However, the woman addressed said that he had 'turned away from spirit' and that he would hear 'nothing of spirit'. By this time she was near to tears. 'He will not let me speak of it,' she said. I was told afterwards that both the woman addressed and her husband had previously taken lessons from Mrs Scott in spirit mediumship. The next woman addressed had an educated voice and often queried the message which was given her and asked for it to be expanded. She was told that she attracted children of all colours around her, red, black, white and yellow. She replied that she knew this. A man was 'given' to her who had died of cancer. She volunteered the information that it was her husband who had died of cancer of the intestines. She was then told that she had the power to cure someone of cancer by spirit healing and she received this information with a solemn gratitude.

Next, a man was addressed. He was uncommunicative and had a fixed, cynical smile. He was asked whether engineering meant anything to him. Instead of the customary response which would either be 'no', or 'yes, my brother was an engineer,' he said, 'I know what the word "engineering" means, if that's what you mean.' The word 'tuberculosis' received the same kind of unhelpful response. This rather vexed Mr

Scott. She said, 'We seem to be at sixes and sevens here.' Eventually she asked him whether he believed in spiritualism or not and established that he did. She told him that he had great psychic power himself. He replied that he knew that he was well-endowed, and that he had himself been a healer several years ago. Mrs Scott then said that since they both believed in the same thing they had nothing to argue about. She told him to warn someone he knew of the possibility of a hand accident at work. She also told him that someone in his family had died of tuberculosis. Finally, she said that with him she had the impression that she was in a small room, the walls of which were closing in. She kept on repeating the word 'strange', assuring the mysterious stranger of her willingness to help and asking him to come again. Mrs Scott then began addressing another lady but almost immediately returned to the previous man. She said, 'I can't leave you, sir.' In all her years as a medium she had never yet had such a strange feeling as she did with this man. As she kept repeating these words to herself the entire congregation broke into song. The hymn began with the words: 'How strange it is on the farther shore.'

After this rather disturbing incident a woman was addressed. She looked tired and ill and was wearing a pink hat. She was told that she had visited someone in hospital and that although it seemed serious the person concerned would get better. She was also very gently told not to cry.

Tom, the secretary of the church, was then addressed and received his usual brief message of encouragement from spirit. He was also told to look after his head and to wear a hat.

Finally, Mrs Scott received a message concerning gangrene. She asked whether anyone could help her disentangle the message which was eventually located as belonging to one particular woman. She was told that an acquaintance of hers had had her toes removed. She was then asked whether the word 'amputation' meant anything to her, to which she replied that of course it did, since her friend had had her toes amputated. She was then told that she had another friend who had been in hospital 'with the stomach' and that she would have to return to hospital for the same reason. With this final message the service was closed.

Second service in Park Street (March 1969)

When I arrived the room was in semi-darkness and only six people had arrived. Mrs Daimler said that the electricity had gone and she was not sure whether or not there would be a meeting. Mrs Roberts had gone to telephone the electricity board. The room was cold, dark and miserable. Attempts at conversation fizzled out repeatedly. Each person appeared sadly isolated now that the purpose of their coming had been removed. Mr Walter tried to play the organ but seemed to have forgotten all the tunes. A few tried to sing.

By 7.20 p.m. about twenty people had gathered. Mrs Daimler decided to start the service despite the failure of the electricity. Mrs Trigg, the medium for the evening, found two candles. We began, as always, with the healing hymn.

Mrs Trigg appeared better educated than previous mediums, but she also appeared to be in a more complete state of possession. She began the sermon very briskly by saying: 'Good evening, I am Dr Oscar.' However, 'sermon' is a misleading word. Her style was more reminiscent of a lecture given by a pompous old professor to a group of medical students. Mrs Trigg was possessed by a bewildering succession of spirits. In fact, the succession was so rapid that it was seldom possible to establish the denotation of the word 'I'. The spirits who seemed to spend the greatest amount of time with her were Dr Oscar, Aunty Mary and Aunty Doris. Both aunties had previously been called Mary and Doris. However, they had grown up in the spirit world and were now aunties. Mrs Trigg used the term 'we' to refer to herself and the collectivity of the spirit people. The term 'you' referred to all those not in the first category. She would frequently say, 'You, earth people'. Very often Mrs Trigg would give such concrete and detailed descriptions that it was difficult to decide whether she was speaking of the earth or spirit world. For example, she would say, 'The other week when I attended a lecture given by a famous doctor in Australia. . . .' It was not until some minutes later when she explained that distance presented no obstacles to spirit people, that I realized that she was not referring to the earth world. Mrs Trigg also described various complicated instruments used in healing. One such instrument resembled a barometer and it measured vulnerability and, hence, the correct combination of rays of different colours needed to produce a beneficial effect. Some rays were harmful and others beneficial. Bad healers and bad spirit doctors might use bad rays to harm people. However, good healers, like good earth doctors, were always working to improve their knowledge, especially their knowledge of rays. Dr Oscar was, in fact, a medical electrician rather than a doctor, being particularly concerned with rays.

Many of the spirit doctors had been trained to act as helpers to the healers whilst they were still children. Last time a count had been made there were sixty such child spirit doctors. The children loved wearing white overalls, white socks and white shoes. Now that they had grown up, many of them had left this group to attach themselves to other healers.

During this lecture Mrs Daimler opened her eyes several times to look at Mrs Trigg. She was obviously perturbed by the content of the service. Towards the end the earth electrician arrived and had to walk through the room. Although Mrs Trigg had previously stated that Aunty Mary would not be disturbed if the electricians came, Mrs Daimler suggested that the sermon be interrupted and a short hymn sung. This seemed to be in the nature of a rite of purification.

Mrs Trigg's talk had lasted for so long that she had very little time left for messages. Five people were addressed. A dark-haired woman, with a sad face, was given a baby boy carried by a little girl of about nine. The baby boy was her own child and she was told not to grieve for it. She would soon feel its cheek pressed against hers.

Another lady was given a grill. This was a symbol. It symbolized a 'mental decision' she would soon have to make. She would be faced with a choice of either becoming a hard business woman or of taking 'the softer option'. The spirits wanted her to take the softer option.

Mrs McDermot, the lady who always receives healing for rheumatoid arthritis, was 'given' a tall, strong-looking policeman. He had his hat under his arm having just come from a funeral. Mrs McDermot said she could not place the funeral although she knew the policeman. She said that she would 'take it home' with her.

I was told that I would work for spiritualism in the future in the field of psychometry.

A gentleman in the back row was given a policeman in the army. Sometimes this man used to wear uniform and sometimes he did not. He was more of a detective really. This detective would be able to help the gentleman in his quest for the truth.

The service ended at 8.30 p.m. There was no healing as the electricity had not been restored.

Third service in Park Street (March 1969)

Mrs Beecham took the service, which was attended by about forty people and there were many who were strangers to me. Mrs Beecham is a well-sized, flourishing woman in late middle-age. Her face has a dreamy stare, but she occasionally breaks out into a smile of unexpected warmth and directness. Her voice, in contrast to her looks, is deep and masculine. It seems to rise from deep down, whilst her word-endings seem to be lost for want of strength. Her accent and manner of speaking both give the impression of being borrowed from another social class.

Mrs Beecham's sermon was long and dramatic and commanded the highest degree of involvement both from herself and the congregation. It was begun by a reading from a book on the nature of life after death. This claimed that we do not live a different kind of life after death but that our true selves emerge. Just as 'the child is father of the man,' so after death we become what we truly are now. Mrs Beecham said we were 'bruised and hurt in the birth pangs of self-realization'. She spoke of 'the corridors of torture and despair' along which we must travel. In passing she mentioned people who 'lend their intellects to government', of poets who 'commune in little circles', of artists who 'seek the true light of the self'. The word 'reality' was a favourite with her. The sermon ended at the highest point of emotional intensity. Mrs Beecham, with arms outstretched and voice emerging in a series of cavernous rumblings, proclaimed, 'Death is no mystery. We want to find our real, real, real selves.' The unanimous response from the congregation was 'God bless you, sister!' and comments of 'Isn't she wonderful!' were heard from several parts of the room.

We sang another hymn and then came to that part of the service called 'the proof of survival'. Seven people were addressed. The first was a handsome, upright middle-aged man with a rich melodious singing voice. Mrs Beecham said that she could see 'building up' behind him a man of the masonic order. He was wearing ribbons around his waist or neck. No answer. He has been wanting to get in touch with you so hard. You have found it impossible to ignore this. You have been trying to brush this thing away, but it has proved impossible. This gentleman of the masonic order was helping to shape your true self, to twine the blue strings together to arrive at a truer light. The blue strings of the aura would win. She was seeing a trumpet circling above his head. Did he belong to a physical circle? No, but he did belong to a musical circle. She was seeing an unfinished script of music, and hearing rich melodious music in a blade of grass. She left him with the words, 'I could stay with you for ever, sir!'

A lady in the front row was then spoken to. Mrs Beecham got a feeling of being unable to breathe, as though a shield had come down over her face and neck. She did not know whether this was physical or mental suffering and grief. A man from the spirit world was telling her to say the words, 'I am preparing a place for you.'

Mrs Beecham was now getting a girl of about twelve years

old who had recently been run over by a car. Would anyone know of such a case? The lady behind me had heard of such a case, although the child was not related to her. This girl was now laughing and happy. Would the lady please find out whether this child's attention had been rapt in listening to music on a small radio when she was run over? Would the same lady know of a 'Willie'? Yes. Her husband. Had he died of a chest condition? Yes. Was it true to say that she was now in a state where she could not speak, where she did not know whether she was coming or going, and could not decide either for or against a thing? Yes, true. Did she know of a dressmaker who had passed to spirit? Yes. Was this dressmaker able to make very elegant and beautiful clothes? Yes, she was a court dressmaker. Mrs Beecham was being shown a most beautiful white wedding dress with a wonderful headdress of little flower buds. Perhaps this signified a betrothal! Would the lady know of anyone who had died with a dislocated hip? Yes, the mother of a lady in the front row. Would she know of anyone who had died of a throat condition? Yes, her husband. Mrs Beecham was being shown a pen. Was it true that her husband could not speak before he died and had to communicate in writing? Did she know of a document he had had to sign shortly before his death? Was it true that recently a piece of unexpected treachery had been revealed to her? Yes. That she was now having to deal with something very embarrassing which was causing her a lot of worry and financial stress? Yes. Well, things would change and the problem would resolve itself after Easter. Mrs Beecham would like to give her a red rose from the spirit world.

Did anyone know of a Bill Harris who had passed to spirit? A lady sitting in the front claimed to know him. Did he have a little moustache and a twinkle in his eye? Yes, that's him. Bill was standing very close to the lady now. Was it true that she had had more help from the spirit world during the last week than she ever dreamed possible? Yes. Mrs Beecham had to give her a bunch of the most beautiful forget-me-nots. They were as blue as the blue of the lady's eyes. And violets, and snowdrops, and lily of the valley and pink carnations: 'A bouquet from the stream of the precious elements of truth.'

Would anyone know of a person who had been involved in an accident and had broken his spine? The tired-looking lady claimed this message. It was her brother. Was he involved in a car crash? No, in the bombing during the war. Was she feeling tired? Yes. For some reason Mrs Beecham saw the flowers scattered all over the floor with this lady. She did not know what had caused it. Her mother was standing behind her and telling her to think hard but to say little. Not to speak her mind straight out. Would she know what was meant? Yes (smiling).

A vigorous, plump woman was addressed next. Mrs Beecham was getting a black mourning veil for some reason. Did she know of someone who had had an abdominal condition? Who had had an operation there? Who was so tired he could not speak; he could just see the curtains drawn around his bed? Yes. Did he cry out the names 'Alice' and 'Mary' before he died? 'Yes, bless you, sister!'

Fourth service in Park Street (April 1969)
There were about twenty-five people present with the usual female majority and a handful of men. Disappointingly, there were only six or so people whom I recognized. The rest were new to me. Mrs Board had brought her son, a lively self-assured young man of about twenty. She was sitting behind me and tapped me gently on the shoulder to say, 'We missed you, but we knew you couldn't come,' the implication being that I would not willingly abandon the meetings.

Mrs Daimler was not there and the task of presiding over the meeting was left to Mr Dear. He asked us to co-operate by setting up good thought vibrations in order that we should be blessed with 'a rich spiritual harvest'. Most mediums, and especially Mr Dear, take an obvious delight in the use of unusual combinations of word-sounds and patterns. One thing which mediums may have in common is that they may all be 'frustrated linguists'.

A Mr Dresden from Neartown was the medium for the evening. He reminded one of a sad looking walrus. He was about sixty-five with a neat silvery moustache. He wore a mustard-coloured waistcoat. He spoke, like Mrs Beecham before him, with a mixture of accents, depending on the word which was being pronounced. One accent was a regional one which I could not place and the other was exaggeratedly upper-class.

Mr Dresden's theme was on the contrast between the unchanging realm of the spirit world and the change and decay of the earth world. This is a theme which is popular in the sermons and occurs frequently in one form or another. The spirit world was referred to in terms of the unchanging values of love, truth and beauty. The material world, on the other hand, was one characterized by pain, lust and the greed for power. A true spiritualist was one who was continuously sensitive to the eternal values and was not led astray by earthly values. For in the spirit world all these things would fall away and we would have to face ourselves as we were, 'good, bad or indifferent'.

As an illustration of the changing nature of the earth world, Mr Dresden cited the example of the younger generation who no longer believed that Christ died for our sins and that Christ would punish us if we were wicked. This statement led Mr Dear to raise his eyebrows, presumably because the idea that Christ died for our sins is explicitly rejected by official spiritualist doctrine. However, despite this disagreement, Mr Dresden was thanked just as profusely at the end of the sermon for his 'inspiring words'. The free-will offering was taken at the end of the sermon, although it is customary for it to be taken at the very end of the service.

After the collection Mr Dresden embarked upon the 'proof of survival'. He first addressed an elderly gentleman who was accompanied by two ladies, both middle-aged. Mr Dresden said, 'I should like to come to the gentleman over there. You, sir.' These words had an obviously disturbing effect on the man concerned for he immediately started breathing quickly and had difficulty in making his voice audible. The women with him, on the other hand, found the encounter with the spirit world much less of a strain and responded eagerly by nudging each other and nodding their heads. This seems to be a difference in response which is common. Men tend to be more embarrassed when addressed by spirits and more secretive about themselves. Women are much more responsive, both in giving information about themselves and by being more ready to accept messages.

There was a gentleman standing behind the elderly man who was stroking his beard much as he had done in life. The spirit would be in his seventies. He was shorter than Mr Dresden but of much the same build. He was a firm, resolute character, and the man addressed should try to follow his example. Was there an anniversary in March? Yes. The gentleman's mother was there asking Mr Dresden to give him some white chrysanthemums. Flowers were, Mr Dresden said, the medium through which spirits expressed themselves. Very frequently spirits would appear before one, if one gazed long enough into a flower.

His 'lady companion' was then addressed. There was a condition of anxiety hanging round about her. However, she should not worry too much about this as it would pass in the near future. Did she suffer with the lower part of her body? No reply. This was an open circle so he did not want to go into the details but the condition would also clear up.

Another middle-aged lady in the row in front of the previous two was then addressed. Would she understand what was meant if he were to say that there was a state of anxiety connected with the home? Yes. This anxiety was directed towards a younger person. She was also in a state of uncertainty with regard to this problem, if he could put it that way. Yes. One moment she was saying 'yes' and the next moment she was saying 'no'. She should cast this thing out of her mind. During the past she had done all she could. More, in fact, than could reasonably be expected of her. No one can do more than that. Instead she should now learn to think about herself. For there was a condition round about her which could cause her some anxiety and which would need attention.

Next a lady in her forties was addressed. This person had started coming to the meetings around the same time as I. Initially, she had uniformly black hair which then turned blonde and was now silver-grey. Was there 'younger life' around her? Yes. Were there in fact two younger lives? Yes. There was strain and rivalry between these two lives? The lady said she could not for the moment place this message. This strain was, however, there even if the lady was not aware of it. She was being warned of it because if she were to become sensitive to this tension it would cause her considerable heart-ache.

Mrs Board's son was addressed. Mr Dresden was getting a pair of scales. These were in the nature of a symbol indicating the fact that there was something in the balance in the life of this young man. To this Mr Dresden got the reply 'possibly' given in a rather clipped and detached voice. He should carry on with what he was doing and not make a choice at present. It was difficult but it was worth it and he would in the end be rewarded amply for his endeavours.

Mr Dresden ended fifteen minutes early, apologizing and saying that he had recently been feeling 'under the weather'.

Fifth service in Park Street (May 1969)
A large congregation of over forty people had assembled and the singing was very loud. Ethel and Mrs Russell from the developing circle were both there. A Mrs Star took the service and Mrs Ellen presided. Mrs Star had a girlish voice, which cracked with emotion. Her face was frequently contorted with nervous tremors and twitches. Her sparsely distributed teeth and hair are an ill-match for her naïvely pleading voice. She has made the same efforts at cultural sophistication noted in some of the previous speakers.

Mrs Star referred collectively to the spirit world as 'we'. 'We have not come to preach to you', she said, 'but to talk with you.' Despite this claim she must have preached for a good half-an-hour. She spoke of faith in the life after death and referred to Matthew 24, where the disciples failed to recognize Jesus after he had risen from the dead. She said, 'Methinks that things have not changed very much. Methinks there are many now who see Him, yet do not see Him.' Speech affectations such as 'methinks' are frequent with spiritualists; they can become irritating.

There were only five messages and they were short. Mrs Star ended by saying, 'The power is still alive around and about me, but my voice is cracking up.'

A lady from Northton (an industrial outlying area of Welshtown) in the back row was addressed first. There was an old lady with very large, beautiful eyes building up behind her. This old lady was connected to her on her mother's side and was very fond of her. She was telling Mrs Star of a condition of anxiety which was round about her; of a heavy burden that she had had to bear, the strain of which was beginning to tell on her physical condition. The anxiety was connected with a younger life and in order that the situation should improve she should buy a tonic. I am not sure that this message was fully understood or accepted, although the lady in question is usually receptive to spirit messages.

Next an overweight lady from Northton was addressed. Mrs Star was getting a condition of total depletion with her. The condition concerned a man and it was, furthermore, deteriorating. An old man with a pipe was telling her to do something about it. This condition, which I think concerned her husband, had been brought out in the same form many times before. I was always surprised at this woman's responsiveness and gratitude when the content of the messages was so uniformly pessimistic and unenlightening.

Next Mrs Star asked whether anyone could place the name 'Jack'. Three ladies offered to do so, including Mrs Russell from the developing circle. Eventually Jack was allocated to a lady in the front row. Had she had a disappointment or a setback recently? Yes. Would it be true to say that she had had a rebuke? Silence. Or rather that she had tried at something very hard but that it had come to no avail? No.

It was then decided that the message had been given to the wrong person and it was then transferred to a lady a few rows back whose situation fitted more neatly. Would this lady know a Mary? Yes. And Elizabeth? Yes. 'I'm on the right vibration then.' And a William? Yes.

Frank was then addressed. There was an elderly man building up behind him. This man did not say much but he thought a great deal. In fact, he had a marvellous personality. Incidentally, Frank himself fits rather well into this image of the strongly thoughtful, silent type. Frequently messages seem to come from spirits, who according to the descriptions given of them, could be thought of as spiritual counterparts or replicas of those for whom the messages are intended. This elderly man was telling Mrs Star that Frank had the most marvellous and inspired thoughts which he should write down. They were much too complicated for Mrs Star to understand, but they would be of great benefit to humanity.

David was addressed. The whole of the front row where he was sitting was bathed in a blue healing light. Had he tried a new method of healing? Yes. There would be a small obstacle in his way but he would be able to overcome it. Personally, Mrs Star thought that the power of healing was the most marvellous gift that God could give to any human being.

The atmosphere and conduct of these services is an essential ingredient of the spiritualist movement. This description of some of these services, therefore, provides the setting in which the performers play their parts. The following sections describe some of the main characters.

Edna

Edna is one of the 'regulars' at King Street. However, although she attends regularly, she does not 'really belong' to King Street. She is a marginal character both in terms of her contribution to the church and in terms of her physical handicaps. Edna is both lame and deaf. She is about sixty-five and lives in a terraced house a few minutes' walk from King Street. She comes every week but never arrives before the service is drawing to a close. She times her entry precisely to coincide with the last five minutes of the service before tea is served. She is universally respected and loved and her belated presence is a necessary, if formally unacknowledged, element in the proceedings. Edna used to be a popular and much travelled 'platform-worker', taking services in churches throughout South Wales. However, her current talents are not strictly orthodox by spiritualist standards. Edna enjoys 'second sight', reads palms and crystal balls and is adept in psychometry. These are not the usual tools of a spiritualist medium in South Wales. Her gifts appear to be 'magical' rather than spiritual. However, she is allowed to practise these arts in King Street after the service has ended. Whilst other women are drinking tea, discussing the service and airing their personal problems, Edna puts her services at the disposal of those most in need. Newcomers are presented to her and the introduction is made in such terms as to make it quite plain that she is regarded as someone very special. It is the custom to slip her surreptitiously a few silver coins, which she receives with a standard response of subdued surprise. Not only is she remunerated for her individual counselling services, she is also given tea and bread and butter at no extra charge. This is in contrast to everyone else, for whom a charge is made for tea. In all, Edna seems to be a highly prized, although foreign, element in the group.

Miss Ryecroft

Miss Rose Ryecroft is in some ways also a marginal character. She is a small, shrivelled woman in her mid-seventies, and she is a regular attender at many services. When she first stood up to take a service she struck me as a pathetic figure, extremely thin, fragile and ugly. It is said that she is a hunch-back because of the beatings which she received from her foster mother as a child. Her voice is high-pitched and grating. She has a habit of clasping the hands of all those who come within her reach in a nervous and obstinate grip. The compensatory aspect of spiritualism is especially apparent in her. Frequently

she finds herself alone in the centre of the room in a complete
social vacuum. She stands unsupported and swaying slightly,
with her mouth open, exposing one lonely tooth. Suddenly,
she raises her arm to point at someone across the room and to
deliver a message. She thus creates a spiritual link when otherwise she would be alone.

Rose is also very nearly blind. At one service, which she was
taking, she wanted to make 'a testimony to the power of
spirit'. As everyone knew, she had been blind for six years, but
that afternoon she had been in the kitchen when behind her
she had heard the words: 'Take the pledge.' She did not know
what the words meant or what kind of a pledge this was. She
therefore, had to have faith. She had taken a small Bible from
the kitchen drawer and read Matthew 17 in its entirety. This
was something she had been unable to do for the last six years.
At this point Rose had difficulty in holding back her tears. She
asked the congregation to sing an uplifting song for her before
she continued any further. We began singing 'Nearer my God
to Thee', which gave her a chance to regain her self-control.

Rose frequently opens a service by asking the congregation to
extend their love to her. Indeed, she looks very much in need
of it. Although sometimes seen in King Street, Rose attends
all the services in Park Street, largely perhaps because her
small terraced house is within walking distance of the church.
However, although she has a widely established reputation for
great spiritual power she has no formal position in Park Street.
This is a source of much tension and insecurity for her. This is
most in evidence on Saturday evenings when an 'open circle'
is held in Park Street. The name is descriptively accurate in
that all are admitted to the circle and all those present are
encouraged to develop their mediumistic powers and give
messages. In practice, however, it is only the well-established
mediums, such as Rose and Mrs Daimler who give messages.
Usually such meetings develop into spiritual battle-grounds,
with each medium trying to give more 'true' messages. Thus
Rose and Mrs Daimler give messages in turn, each trying to
encroach a little more on the other's time. Rose is especially

insistent that her messages be accepted as true. She says: 'Give me the truth as I have given it to you,' thus implying that a rejection of the message would be equivalent to lying.

Mrs Daimler

Mrs Daimler is a less marginal character and is less easily described. In this respect she is like the majority of spiritualists about whose lives outside of the spiritualist meetings one learns very little. She is well-known as a medium, as well as being the president of Park Street. She is in her sixties and has been twice married. Her second husband died of cancer in the autumn of 1970. Although he was a Methodist and did not have spiritualist beliefs he nevertheless came to spiritualist meetings, and frequently acted as organist. Mrs Daimler claims that before his death he saw the truth and was converted to spiritualism. His death appears to have had only a small effect on Mrs Daimler. Although looking a little older and slightly shrunken, Mrs Daimler was taking services a week after his death. Her sorrow appears to have increased both her prestige and her perceptive and mediumistic powers. In this Mrs Daimler is typical of most mediums whose claims to give help to others in suffering are based on their own encounters with pain and misfortune.

This chapter is concerned with the part played by illness in spiritualist belief and practice. It also examines spiritualists' experience of and response to pain. Spiritualists lend themselves particularly well to such a study since they consider themselves beset by a variety of disabilities and are preoccupied with the problem of suffering and its communication. To illustrate this there is the example of how Leah reacted to a series of difficulties arising from her family situation and the terms in which she subsequently described these to spiritualist meetings.

Leah is in her early fifties and married to a builder and decorator. They have three adolescent children. She is a large, red-faced woman with a loud voice and an air of energy about her, despite her avowals to the contrary. She is a member of King Street and has been participating in meetings for some twenty years. During the time of my field-work Leah experienced a variety of problems each of which reinforced the others. Over the past few years her husband has engaged in increasingly heavy drinking which takes him out of the house on most nights of the week. This segregation of activities accentuates the separation between Leah and her husband and minimizes the communication between them which at best has not been good. More drinking meant less money and thus reduced the likelihood of moving out of the small and cramped terrace in which they lived to more comfortable quarters. In addition to the increasing alienation between husband and wife and increasing financial difficulties, Leah's health began to show the effects of the strain under which she was working. Tiredness and inability to concentrate permeated her life. Severe back pain made housework more difficult. Self-diagnosed anaemia and high blood pressure provided the explanation for her general weariness and inability to cope. In turn, this bad state of health had repercussions on her relationship with her children at a stage in their development when they were particularly tiring and rebellious. This series of difficulties was relayed back to spiritualist meetings both in the course of informal chat and during services when messages of advice were received from spirit and elaborated upon. Leah in this case clearly saw her physical ailments as being inextricably woven into a wider fabric composed of her other social and personal problems.

This brief history points to the necessity of defining the standpoint from which illness is being considered. Both laymen and sociologists recognize a distinction between a pathological condition and attributed sickness which may or may not have a basis in real pathology. Furthermore, this sickness may be a self-attribution or may be attributed by the family or other social group. Medical sociologists have, in fact, been concerned with the divergence between the incidence of pathology, such as might be uncovered by a screening programme, and socially defined sickness which entails the adoption of the 'sick role'. For example, different social classes react differently to the same bodily symptom. A working-class person is consistently less likely to regard a particular symptom as meriting the doctor's attention, and as being indicative of sickness. For example, Koos (1954) presented a number of 'Class I', 'Class II' and 'Class III' people with a hypothetical symptom such as a 'lump in the abdomen' and asked them whether or not they would report this symptom to the doctor. He found that whilst 92 per cent of the 'Class I' would take the symptom to the doctor, only 34 per cent of the 'Class III' would do so. Thus the definitions of sickness and health, whether or not these are 'real' in the sense of according with the pathologist's diagnosis, are important in that they are likely to have real consequences.

Therefore, from the point of view of the sufferer the distinction between sickness and real pathology is meaningless, since the experience of pain is not affected by its basis. The spiritualist sufferer is concerned with his experience of pain irrespective of whether this has a basis in physiological disorder or psychological and social conflict. As far as the spiritualist is concerned spirit healing is effective in that he or she no longer has pain and no necessity is felt for further treatment.

Given this approach to sickness the introduction of the term 'sociosomatic' is particularly useful with regard to my material. Illness which does not have a basis in real pathology has usually been labelled 'psychosomatic' and has been interpreted as stemming from conflicts in the individual psyche. I argue that in many cases this is an inappropriate label and that the term 'sociosomatic' should be substituted with greater descriptive accuracy.[1] Reproductive disorders among women are typically among those most readily described as being of psychosomatic origin. I have argued elsewhere (1970) that statements about reproductive disorders and menstrual processes are symbolic statements about social roles and relationships. Menorrhagia, for example, can in many instances be looked upon as a 'housewife's sickness'. It is, therefore, of 'sociosomatic' rather than of psychosomatic origin.

Returning to spiritualists, many of their complaints are interwoven with difficult social or marital situations. This is illustrated by the way in which illness is presented within the spiritualist group as one among a number of difficulties with which spiritualists have to contend. This heterogeneity in the presentation of misfortune is echoed in an eclecticism in explaining sickness. No one explanatory model predominates. Social, psychological and organic possibilities are considered as exerting a causal influence on sickness. Similarly, there is an eclectic approach to treatment. Spirit healing, herbal remedies, psychological insight and sometimes suggestions for social manipulation of difficult situations are each considered as methods worth trying.

[1] I am grateful to Mr John Komarov for suggesting the term.

This eclectic or 'sociosomatic' approach to sickness finds its focal point of expression in the spiritualist concept of 'aura'. Everybody is thought to have an aura. It is half-physical, half-spiritual, like a rainbow surrounding the body. Although not visible to the uninitiated it can be seen by 'sensitives' or those who are spiritually developed. A person's aura acts as a barometer measuring social, psychological or physical balance and imbalance. This balance and harmony, or their lack, are reflected in colour. A good aura is white, blue or purple. A bad aura is a dark colour, especially red. The colour of the aura can be affected for the worse by an imbalance or state of conflict at any level, whether it be at the level of social conflict and strain or at the level of organic pathology. Blue is described as the 'healing colour' and is especially highly valued. The aura of a healthy and well-balanced individual, who is at peace with himself and others, is blue. Occasionally, when members of a spiritualist group are 'in tune' with one another and are temporarily freed from misfortune, a blue light is seen surrounding the circle.

Much of spiritualist activity is concerned with healing and giving advice about sickness, which is described more fully later. However, before turning to the details of these activities a summary of the types of complaints managed by spiritualism and their relationship with orthodox medicine is necessary.

Unlike Christian Science, spiritualism does not attempt to assert its supremacy over orthodox medicine. Spiritualists are seldom discouraged from seeing their doctor and they are rarely given advice which contradicts that of the doctor. Spiritualism does not see itself as an alternative to orthodox medicine but rather as its complement. It fills in the gaps and smooths over the inadequacies of more orthodox treatment methods. Thus it does not deal with a peculiar sector of illness: it has a contribution to make towards the management of all sickness. Most frequently spirit healing aims to increase a person's overall vitality, zest and resistance towards disease and the strains and stresses of life. In other words, one need not have a specific complaint to be able to benefit from spirit healing. However, healing is also given for specific complaints which have either been previously diagnosed by a doctor or are diagnosed within the spiritualist setting by spirit. In such instances spirit healing is always thought to help, in that it alleviates pain, and is sometimes thought to cure. There are many first-hand accounts of such cures. Blindness, stomach ulcers, kidney stones have disappeared, it is claimed, by spirit healing. Thus within the context of spiritualist ideology there is a tradition of curing and plenty of evidence of its success. Whether or not such cures would be recognized by 'scientific' medicine did not form part of my research interest, in that I was concerned with whether spiritualists themselves considered themselves to be cured. Thus success was judged by their self-assessment of health.

At this point perhaps an account of the structure of the spirit world should be introduced in order to bring out its relationship to earthly suffering. Two words are frequently used. 'Spirit' is commonly used to refer to the mystical, the non-empirical. It is used in such contexts as, for example, 'I am getting a message from spirit,' or, 'Spirit is very strong with you,' or, 'Spirit is protecting you all the way.' Interchangeable with the word 'spirit' in some contexts is the word 'power'. Thus one can correctly say: 'The power is very strong with you.' However, it would not be correct spiritualist usage to say either: 'I am getting a message from power,' or, 'Power is protecting you all the way.' These examples show that 'power' can be used as a synonym for 'spirit' only in contexts where it is most closely related to and intermingled with human beings. Thus where spirit is thought of as a discrete entity, distinct from human beings, it cannot also be referred to as 'power'. However, in contexts where a person has already become an instrument of spirit it is usual and correct to use the term 'power'. In such contexts the word 'power' is not only conventionally correct, it is also literally true. Messages which are agreed to come from spirit are axiomatically true and, therefore, confer great power and prestige on the medium. (There is a similarity with

Middleton's account (1960) of the Lugbara conceptualization of spirit in terms of its remote and immanent aspects. The Lugbara words refer to spirit in its remote aspects as being creative and infinite and to spirit in its immanent aspects as being the cause of pestilence, droughts and famine.) The parallel between the spiritual categories of Welshtown spiritualists and those of the Lugbara is not complete but it is there nevertheless. Although 'power' is not necessarily conceptualized as evil and hence is not the complete equivalent of the Lugbara term, nevertheless there is a distinct value for spirit in its immanent aspect. However, it is only in its immanent aspects that spirit can be bad or produce illness. In other words, the badness of bad spirits is only manifest on those occasions when they possess a person.

Spirits are hierarchically organized, there being a continuous upward movement from the time of death. Communication is usually with the spirits from the lower ranks of the hierarchy. Communication between human beings and the lower spirits constitutes a link of mutual interdependence. Immediately after death spirits find themselves at a 'loose end' in the spirit world and still feel strongly attached to their 'earth conditions'. They are in a state of transition between the living and the dead. This state is ambiguous and, hence, dangerous. Spiritualists are able to help spirits who are trapped in the meshes of their previous existence by performing as mediums and acting out conditions of affliction. Through mediumship such spirits can be released from the previously painful conditions to which they were bound. Acting as instruments of spirits, spiritualists can provide the stage on which the circumstances of dying can be re-enacted. The medium becomes possessed or 'takes on the condition' of a dying person so that, in effect, a death scene is re-enacted in the midst of the spiritualist circle. Thus the spirit in question is freed from the scene of his earthly pain and suffering and allowed to move upwards in the spirit world. Without the ready help of spiritualist mediums, spirits would remain forever fettered to this life. This aspect of spiritualist activity is known as 'rescuing' or 'rescue operations'.

The most difficult 'rescue operations' are notoriously those which involve the spirits of deceased mediums.

The link between the spirit and physical world is one of mutual interdependence and help flows both ways. Human beings are dependent upon spirit for help. This help takes the form of advice about health problems, emotional problems, protection in the face of difficulties and, most important, the power of healing. Such advice is not expected to come from the spirits of the immediately departed. It has been shown that they are themselves helpless. Neither is it thought to come from those spirits who have progressed far in the spirit world. They are no longer concerned with human beings and their material problems. Help is thought to come from those spirits occupying an intermediate position in the spiritual hierarchy. They are neither so involved in 'earth conditions' as to need help themselves, nor so distant as to be completely unconcerned. Perhaps, the easiest way of indicating the scope of the spirit world is to list the categories of spirits which it contains:

(a) There is a vast array of spirits who have ascended into the higher realms of the spirit world. No communication exists with these spirits and, hence, they are seen as an undifferentiated spiritual mass in which little interest is expressed.

(b) The second category in order of spiritual prestige, involves all those spirits who return to give advice. These range from the permanent and reliable spirit-guide to the casual spirit visitor with a single item of advice.

(c) A third large-sized category of spirits covers those who, whilst not malevolent, are themselves in need of comfort and help as a result of some particularly distressing 'earth conditions' which they have experienced and are unable to remove.

(d) A fourth slightly smaller category includes all spirits who have died a violent or painful death. These are the spirits who call the 'rescue operations' of mediums into action. Contact with these spirits requires a high degree of skill and control.

(e) A final category, constituting a sub-category of category (d), contains all those spirits, malevolently disposed, who actively inflict sickness.

Tambiah (1970, p. 316) refers to this final category as those who have 'unnaturally escaped society'. He explains the evil nature of these spirits in the following terms (ibid.):

> The belief in the violent spirit is thus a magnified and dramatized conceptualization of a free-floating malignant force, which, however, does not find an expression as systematized cult behaviour. It represents the theoretical extreme of the concept of an unfulfilled life, the notion being transferred into the notion of an uncontrollable evil.

Thus it can be seen that the scope of spiritual categories is such as to provide an adequate mirror for the varieties of human distress. The range is between distressing conditions—which can be managed with little active display of emotion—to those evoking strong emotional responses and acting out behaviour. It is of interest that in the latter case the distress is located in the spirit world and the human agent is seen as taking on the role of a competent and generous helper.

Most spiritualists admit to physical disabilities. However, they do not regard this as unusual. Sickness, whether chronic, temporary or recurrent, is interwoven with the spiritualists' expectations of life. From this there stems a theme of sadness running through all spiritualist activities. Spiritualists consider themselves different from others not in claiming more illness for themselves, but in their management of it. Thus each occurrence in the medical and emotional history of a spiritualist is a proper object of attention for the entire spiritualist group.

An analogy using the idea of an auction will help to make clear the concerns of spiritualist circles.[1] The central importance of illness emerges from questions which such an analogy suggests. The questions to be asked include the following: What is the bidding for? Who are the auctioneers? In what currency is the bidding made? What rules govern bidding?

At spiritualist meetings bidding is for attention and status

[1] I am grateful to Dr Basil Sansom for suggesting this analogy.

and all spiritualists participate in the bidding. However, the participants are both auctioneers and bidders. Within the space of an evening spiritualists both bestow concern and attention on others and demand it for themselves. The currency is in terms of physical or emotional complaint. However, there are well-defined norms which specify what can and cannot be put up for auction and the manner in which this must be done. Conversation at meetings has as its focus the body and onslaughts on its well-being. Bidding for attention which becomes too frequent is critically received. However, a reserve is set below which bidding for attention is not tolerated. Physical impairment is, thus, almost a pre-condition of eligibility for group membership. Therefore, the degree and nature of participation by members in the activities of the group is controlled.

So far I have described the uses of illness in a spiritualist context. I now want to examine the spiritualist experience of pain and responses to it. Much has been written by sociologists but little by anthropologists about the presentation of illness. Discussion has usually been under the heading of 'the theory of illness behaviour.' Sociologists have aimed to identify social factors which are relevant to the way in which sickness is perceived and which determine the subsequent behaviour of the sick person. Medical sociologists have tried to show how behaviour in sickness is connected with a number of factors other than those relating to the severity or intensity of pain. For example, the values placed on endurance and self-control as opposed to the ready dramatization of pain have been cited already (see for example, Zola, 1966; Zborowski, 1952). Behaviour in sickness has also been related to the social role of the sick person and the way in which the sickness can be accommodated to current obligations (see Robinson, 1971). Such considerations as these have directed attention away from the problem of pain and unease, popularly regarded as being at the very heart of sickness. No doubt this is an attempt to focus attention away from the physical to the social and cultural. However, in the course of this shift of attention a large area belonging to the cultural, namely, the structure of pain experience, has, in fact, been relegated to the biological. Perhaps another reason why the connection between pain and sickness has been neglected is because it is too close and uncomfortable. However, little has been written about the influence which the structure of pain experience has on the presentation of sickness. The problem of examining the cultural and linguistic conventions which determine the perception and expression of pain has been left on one side. More importantly there is no systematic study of how the perception of pain is reflected in subsequent definitions, the management of sickness and healing procedures. A number of interesting questions can be raised which have hitherto been largely of interest to philosophers. Wittgenstein (1963, section 256) for example, was interested in how we learn to identify pains. He asks how we learn to use words to name sensations.

The aim of this chapter is not merely to demonstrate a general concern which spiritualism has with pain, suffering and its management, but to indicate the precise topography and content of spiritualist pain-experience and to relate this to their group activities. One approach is to consider certain key spiritualist rituals and thereby infer the underlying attitudes to pain. A more direct approach considers overtly expressed ideas about pain.

Spiritualist thought is diffused with anxieties about communication, that is, the inability to convey the precise quality of an experience to others and the sense of isolation when faced with pain and suffering. The activities of spiritualist groups express these anxieties. Moreover, the development of mediumistic powers is one of the ways in which the quality of communication between people is improved. It is a way of penetrating the 'inner world' of others as well as the spirit world.

One way of becoming aware of the spiritualist experience of pain and the anxiety about its communication is by briefly considering a philosophical controversy about pain. The problems are definitional. Should pain be defined as a sensation or an emotion? Jeremy Bentham (1789) treated both pains and pleasures as sensations. Francis Herbert Bradley (1888), on the other hand, regarded pains as emotions. Pain, he thought, contributes the feeling-tone to an experience.

How pain is defined determines pain behaviour. Thus given our own linguistic conventions, pain defined as a sensation cannot be shared. One can *have* a pain, itch or throb, but one cannot be said to *know* it and neither can anyone else. Pain defined as emotion, however, relates to suffering. It can be communicated and, hence, shared. This philosophical digression in the middle of an anthropological text is justified if it reveals a variety of definitions of pain and, hence, ways of handling pain.

The teaching of spiritualist mediums involves an implicit awareness of such definitional controversies. On the one hand, they are taught to become possessed or 'to take on a condition'. On the other hand, they are taught to become 'impressed' or 'to listen to spirit'. In possession or taking on a condition, the condition which is taken on is usually a painful one, such as, for example, a back-ache, a migraine or a stomach-ache. This is the condition suffered by one of the members of the spiritualist group or by a spirit whilst it was on the 'earth plane'. However, according to spiritualist theory, this condition may be experienced not only by the sick person but also by the healer and any other spiritualists who are 'sensitives'. By 'taking on conditions' pains can be shared in much the same way as visual or auditory objects can be shared. The pain acquires some of the properties of a physical object, which several people can see, hear or feel at the same time, provided they are favourably situated. Pains taken on by 'sensitives' resemble the blurred contours of physical objects seen in a dim light.

'Listening to' or becoming 'impressed' by spirit is a more complex activity. This procedure requires an active response on the part of the developing medium as opposed to a passive surrendering of one's conscious personality. It is a way of transmitting information and advice from spirit to human beings. Such information and advice relates broadly to the fields of physical sickness and interpersonal relations.

These two types of activities can broadly be described as representing the overtly therapeutic and the didactic elements in spiritualism. More advanced spiritualists usually acquire a 'spirit-guide', that is, a spirit whose connections are confined to one particular spiritualist. Such guides are frequently, though not necessarily, thought to be the spirits of deceased doctors and preachers. As such the healing powers which they are able to confer upon individual spiritualists are especially strong. These spirit-guides resemble the Tallensi ideas about 'good destiny'. Like the good destiny a spirit-guide is not acquired before adolescence. Similarly, it makes its presence felt to the medium through a series of minor accidents (see Fortes, 1959, pp. 41–55).

This description of ritual activities brings out the basically solipsistic nature of the spiritualist world-view. Spiritualists see each other as being rather like Ryle's 'ghost in the machine', each living 'the life of a ghostly Robinson Crusoe' (1949, p. 13). This epistemological outlook is one which, at the emotional level, produces feelings of loneliness and isolation. It is also one which inclines towards seeking help from a mystical source in order to ease communication and overcome epistemological barriers. Most knowledge of others is gained by 'taking on a condition' or by 'listening to spirit'. 'Taking on a condition' means complete identification with the other, in the sense of having their feelings and emotions. The implication is that any other form of acquiring knowledge of the state of mind of others by more empirical, everyday methods is bound to be incomplete, imperfect and, hence, in the long-run, disappointing.

The privacy felt to enclose one's inner world becomes especially hard to tolerate where illness or emotional hardship is involved. This may be because these are situations which most urgently require guidance or rules for understanding and acting, a feature which is conspicuously absent from a private world. However, these attitudes are not only implicitly revealed in certain ritual activities of spiritualists. They are also openly acknowledged. Spiritualists admit to turning to spiritualism 'out of pain and sorrow' and the need to share these.

This view of pain which places it in a domain of logically enforced privacy is one which has implications for the classification of pain and sickness as types of misfortune. Pain isolates and is difficult to communicate. Sickness, by contrast, breaks down this isolation in that diagnoses of sickness enable the individual to see himself as one of a category of sick people.

This difficulty in tolerating the epistemological privacy of pain and the response of spiritualism to pain is particularly interesting and unusual when considered in the light of psychiatric thought. Loss of psychological privacy, in the sense both of sharing thoughts, emotions and feelings and having them controlled by others is taken as indicative of a loss of sanity. According to Laing (1971, p. 36): 'The loss of the experience of an area of unqualified privacy, by its transformation into a quasi-public realm, is often one of the decisive changes associated with the process of going mad. ...' This area of 'unqualified privacy' is, according to Laing, a reflection of the preoccupation with 'the inner/outer, real/unreal, me/not-me, public/private lines' (ibid, p. 34). Traditional psychiatry refers to the loss of the privacy of experience and, hence, of ego boundaries and the identity of the self in terms such as 'ideas of passivity', 'ideas of reference' and 'ideas of influence'. Within the psychiatric frame of reference, such terms are indicative of the psycho-pathological condition of the individual. By contrast, spiritualism encourages such states of mind and they are achieved by mystical means.

The comparison is striking both in terms of the similarities and the dissimilarities which it shows. On the one hand, there is a similarity between the type of experiences sought by spiritualists and the thought patterns diagnosed as 'schizophrenic' by psychiatrists. On the other hand, opposed values are placed upon such experiences according to the context in which they appear. (Difficulties in the interpretation of experiences of loss of privacy become most acute when the same person is both a spiritualist and a psychiatric patient.) Loss of psychological boundaries in the context of the spiritualist circle seem particularly interesting when seen as a variation of the theme of loss of bodily boundaries. Values placed on bodily boundaries and their concomitants in social structure have received much attention (see for example, Douglas, 1970). However, the boundaries of the 'self' and the experience of self have been neglected.

The way in which spiritualists experience pain and illness can be shown in more detail by describing the way in which actual physical complaints are dealt with. The responses to illness can be roughly grouped under three headings, although each response has elements which it shares with the others. The headings are as follows: 'taking on conditions'; 'healing'; 'message-giving'.

In describing the training of spiritualist mediums reference has already been made to 'taking on conditions'. It provides the back-bone or element of continuity for all other spiritualist activities. It is the mystical insight into the ordinarily hidden pains of others.

Spiritualists refer to 'the power of healing' as the greatest gift which spirit can bestow on human beings. Most healers are men, although women can, in principle, become healers too. Spirit healing involves the mystical discovery and identification of pain and sickness. It penetrates other bodies and unearths information otherwise available only to the patient.

It is believed that the healer is only an instrument or receptacle of the healing art of a spirit, frequently the spirit of a deceased doctor. The healer himself usually knows that this possession has taken place by a peculiar tingling sensation in his fingertips. When this sensation is present the healer should place his hands on to that part of a woman's anatomy to which he is guided by spirit. The patient knows that she is receiving this healing power by the intense heat which emanates from the healer's hands and which penetrates her body. This power, although it has physical attributes such as those that cause the sensation of heat to be felt, is itself non-empirical. The presence and the efficacy of the power are established *ex post facto* when health has, in fact, been restored.

At the level of empirical description, spirit healing involves the laying on of hands by the healer to that part of the body which is understood to be the cause of pain. Usually the healer's hands move in gentle stroking motions. Sometimes the healer shakes his hands after each stroke, thus symbolically discarding the sickness that has been drawn out of the patient's body. At sessions which are specifically and exclusively devoted to spirit healing several healers work at the same time. Healers wear white coats and stand or kneel by the patient who is seated on a chair. Each healer has a plastic bowl of water by his side in which he washes his hands after giving healing to each patient. In return, the patient, when he or she feels the healer's hands being placed upon him, says either 'Thank you' or 'Bless you'.

The range of complaints treated by spirit healing is wide. Complaints vary both in their degree of severity and in duration. The efficacy of spirit healing is highly valued. It is believed that the discomfort of chronic complaints such as rheumatoid arthritis can be alleviated through spirit healings. Also that acute conditions such as ulcers, growths and kidney stones can be completely removed.

In so far as messages from spirit relate to pain and sickness they perform a labelling or diagnostic and explanatory service. The content of messages is obtained by 'listening to' or becoming 'impressed' by spirit. This activity is a complex one since it demands an active and creative response on the part of the listener. Part of an aspiring medium's education involves training in the presentation of messages. It is thought that messages should be spiritual not 'material'. They should aim to sum up a person's situation or condition in a highly symbolic or eidetic form.

All spiritualist meetings involve a continuous re-interpretation and reassessment of feelings, motives and relationships, especially in so far as these affect the members' well-being or lack of it. This endless sifting of experience recalls Kafka's description of the Day of Judgment as a 'court in standing session'.

Messages from spirit define conditions involving pain and

suffering in such a way that they can be managed and handled. The sense of privacy and isolation felt by spiritualists to be a necessary corollary of pain gives rise to the demand that the sickness be seen as part of a more general pattern, that it be explained by being seen as one instance of a recurring series of events. In other words, that the painful event be defined and given a symbolic meaning. Detailed probing, both in the course of ordinary conversation and in the course of delivering messages, is made about physical ailments, Such probing is especially apparent during 'the unorganized phase' of the illness (Balint, 1964, p. 2). Frequently it aims at locating the sources of tension in a person's social relationships in so far as these might be responsible for the lack of physical well-being. The establishment of a definitive reality is a mutual undertaking made by the healer and the sufferer and it bears a close resemblance to the process, described by Balint (ibid., pp. 21–36), of bargaining for a diagnosis in terms of 'offers and responses'.

An example of the management of pain and distress, which brings into play the major spiritualist activities, can be presented with reference to one particular woman. *Alice* is a married woman in her early forties who has been a member of a developing circle for sixteen years. Her husband works as an insurance agent, whilst she is a housewife who has no children. Their marriage does not seem to be altogether satisfactory (this is described in greater detail in chapter 4). Her time seems to be taken up with looking after the small terraced house in which they live and nursing a succession of disabilities. Although Alice claims not to have had any major illnesses she has, according to her own self-assessment, always been 'highly strung'. She attributes this to the many 'shocks' she has suffered during her lifetime. The death of her parents when she was in early adulthood is still a source of considerable anxiety and distress to her. Alice's life, although superficially undemanding, requires continued and arduous effort on her part. Such effort is supported and encouraged by the circle.

Throughout her married life Alice has suffered from a series of disabilities. Her health is a constant source of anxiety both to her and to other members of the circle. The weekly meeting of the circle provides a forum at which Alice can describe any new difficulties which have appeared to thwart her peace of mind and to report on the adequacy or otherwise of the coping techniques which have been suggested to her at the previous meeting. She has described herself as 'living with the doctor' for several years. Her complaints are always associated with intense and unbearable pain, such that they force themselves to the forefront of her mind. Her original and long-standing complaint was migraine. This became so severe that it needed nightly calls from her local doctor. At the time when I first met Alice she was suffering from a cyst in the left eye. Shortly afterwards she developed another cyst behind her right ear. This condition involved unbearable pain. It left her weak and incapable during the day and tense and sleepless during the night. Her doctor was, it seems, unable either to relieve the condition or to support her in her suffering. In fact, she was told to forget the cysts. But how could she forget something that literally and metaphorically filled her whole field of vision? Eventually the cysts were surgically removed. Exactly three days later Alice developed a gall-bladder infection. Again she described the pain as being 'unbearable' and 'beyond description'.

These ailments have received different methods of management and treatment from the circle. First, Alice receives healing at almost every meeting. A few days after the development of the gall-bladder infection, Alice received healing from a male member of the circle. By the following morning the condition had cleared and when she went for an X-ray that afternoon, the results were negative. 'Spirit' had already been at work. Alice is also given a great many messages from spirit referring both to her state of mind and to her state of health. Various strategies are suggested as to how she might learn to cope better with her afflictions. Finally, Alice is taught how to relax and become an 'instrument' of spirit by one of the male healers of the group. In sum, Alice's difficulties are listened to, assessed and interpreted by the group and suggestions are made for their management.

The perception of pain and suffering as being, first, essentially private and, hence, divisive, and second, an integral part of life, especially a woman's life, influences not only the specific procedures developed for handling illness but also the setting in which these occur. In this context it is significant that most meetings, especially those which encourage the development of mediumistic powers, form an actual *circle* of sitters.

Like all good symbols the circle is significant at a number of different levels of meaning. First, at the level of social structure it reflects the ideal of equality between the 'sitters' expressed in the frequently repeated maxim: 'We all rise together.' This equality is with respect to access to spiritual power, since it is thought that everyone possesses mediumistic power in a latent, if not manifest, form. Spiritualists themselves say: 'The circle has no beginning and no end; it is perfect. That is why we sit in a circle.' It is thus consciously thought of as a symbol of spiritual perfection. It is also an apt reminder of the permanence and continuity of suffering and pain. Thus, in one sense, the circle can be seen as a reconciliatory device. On the one hand, there is an explicit emphasis on continued spiritual progress summed up in the principle of 'eternal progress open to every human soul', whilst on the other hand, there is a conspicuous lack of any real change in the lives of spiritualist women. Spiritualism can, therefore, be seen as a ritual of reconciliation. The supportive and therapeutic nature of the groups is underlined by the fact that there is little, if any, interaction between the members of a spiritualist group outside that group.

To conclude I want to suggest a cross-cultural approach bearing in mind the associations suggested by this spiritualist material. Is there a correlation between the degree of privacy or publicity felt to surround pain and a corresponding emphasis on mystical or secular methods of diagnosis and cure? The notions of privacy and lack of rule have not previously been singled out as significant concepts in understanding and explaining responses to illness and misfortune, and consideration should be given to this omission.

This chapter shows how ritual, both verbal and non-verbal, involved in spiritualism helps women to accept a traditionally feminine role, which they frequently find frustrating and difficult. For a large number of women at least, spiritualism is a response to conflict-ridden situations with men. These relationships and the conflicts which they generate are reflected in various conditions of affliction within spiritualist meetings. They are reflected in messages of advice from spirit. However, these conflicts manifest themselves in a strikingly concrete way in healing rituals involving a male healer and a female patient. Although men form only a small percentage of the total membership, they provide about half the mediums and nearly all the healers.

Attention is frequently drawn to the high proportion of women at religious meetings. 'Peripheral' spirit possession is no exception and the current literature on the subject sees it as primarily a feminine concern (see for example, Lewis, 1966). The sex composition of spiritualist meetings in Welshtown adds confirmation to this view. Nearly 80 per cent of members are women. However, the small percentage of men are regarded as a welcome and very important element at all meetings. This is apparent from the cries of enthusiasm which their entrance invariably evokes as compared with a woman member. Again, in relation to their small numbers, men receive a higher proportion of messages than women. Finally, spirit healing is predominantly a masculine art. It can be seen, therefore, that both in terms of numbers of men involved and in terms of their role within the movement, spiritualism is not exclusively a female concern. At a more subjective level, meetings without men seem to fall flat. This is noticed by all those present and their absence is sadly lamented. At such meetings conversation is desultory and spirit remains remote. Such meetings tend to close earlier than usual.

The presence of a male minority has been underplayed in the anthropological literature on the subject of 'peripheral' spirit possession. Lewis (1966, p. 318), for example, refers to spirit possession in Somaliland as 'this characteristically woman's affliction'. Men, in so far as they enter the picture, are referred to as 'other depressed categories'. Simon Messing (1958, p. 1120), writing about spirit possession in Ethiopia, says: 'Most patients are married women who feel neglected in a man's world, in which they serve as hewers of wood and haulers of water. . . .' Grace Harris (1957) also comes down firmly in favour of classifying spirit possession as a woman's concern among the Kenyan Taita. A man may own houses, cattle and land, whilst a woman's only complete possession is her body. It is, therefore, the only thing which can effectively be the object of mystical attack—hence the epidemiology of spirit possession.

It is clear that the epidemiology of spirit possession in these societies cannot be understood without referring to the status of women. Spirit possession may indeed be a 'characteristically woman's affliction' in the societies in which it has been studied. However, the current literature on the subject should not blind us to the fact that in South Wales it is not exclusively a female concern and that male membership does not necessarily consist of effeminate men or 'pseudo-males'. Nor are the women necessarily 'pseudo-females' as Henry James implied. In other words, our approach needs to be such that we are able to treat men as a distinct category and not necessarily to assimilate them into the category of deprived women.

For many women spiritualism is a response to conflict-ridden situations with men. These conflicts are re-enacted and controlled within the spiritualist circle. More specifically, there is a ritual re-enactment of male-female roles ideally conceived.

Such ritual requires the presence of male members. Thus women's relationships with men within the circle provide a model which other real-life relationships try to imitate. Before giving ethnographic evidence in support of the view that spiritualism is a response to conflict, a more formal point needs to be made in support of this thesis.

Possession in the societies studied by the anthropologists mentioned earlier makes itself known through illness. A possessed woman is nearly always an ill woman, although an ill woman need not be possessed. In fact, a woman discovers that she is possessed and is able to identify the spirit possessing her by becoming ill. This is not the exact case in Welshtown, where possession is not usually thought of as an attack, neither does the possessed herself become ill as the result of possession. It is not, therefore, a means of exercising 'mystical aggression'. This does not mean to say that the aetiology of illness is theoretically impossible or even unheard of by Welshtown spiritualists. Such things have been known to occur and the importance of taking precautions against the possibility of their recurrence is stressed. However, such cases are unusual and a distinction is made between 'ordinary' possession and possession by evil spirits. It is only the evil spirits who cause harm to the possessed woman or 'instrument'. However, the harm which can be wrought in such cases is more often mental than physical, although both types of damage can occur. Most frequently, possession by evil spirits results in insanity. Hence, leaders of developing circles lay great emphasis on the importance of controlling the spirits that have access to one's mind. For this reason they advise would-be mediums never to 'sit' alone, since in doing so they lay themselves open to evil influence. Thus it is generally known that small children are most open to invasion by evil spirits, as they have least control over their minds. It is said that their 'doorkeepers' have not yet awakened. Conversely, there is a connection between successful possession by spirit and the degree to which a person is subject to control. Hence, children and 'neurotics' make bad spiritualists and are advised not to attend meetings or developing circles. Many mismanaged cases of possessed children have been cited who are now, tragically, confined to mental hospitals. Although ostensibly classified as insane, they are not insane according to spiritualists, but merely possessed by insane or evil spirits. Indeed, psychiatrists have come under frequent attack for not allowing spiritualists access to the inmates of mental hospitals.

This mapping out of the areas of highest vulnerability to possession by evil spirits underlines the significance which spiritualists attribute to the concept of control. Thus a child is thought to be lacking in control and discipline as opposed to an adult. A person is more likely to escape control when alone than when not alone. Finally, an experienced medium who has had a guided course in communication with spirit is more likely to be in control than the uninitiated. These paired concepts of adult/child, alone/not alone, experienced/inexperienced can each be seen as an expression of the preoccupation with control. For example, great emphasis is laid on the necessity of controlling one's misfortunes and ailments, in short, one's life-situation, both by manipulating symbols and by the choice of spirits allowed to enter the circle.

Thus, Welshtown spiritualists do, in fact, recognize the possibility of a connection between possession and illness or misfortune. Much more frequently, however, possession takes a different form. The two most common forms of possession are either 'taking on a condition' or being 'impressed', already referred to in chapter 3. In the latter case, the mind is conceived of as a wax tablet upon which images or visual and auditory messages imprint themselves.[1] In the former case of 'taking on a condition' the possessed woman does, indeed, suffer the symptoms of an ill person, namely those symptoms suffered by the spirit whilst it was still alive. Frequently there is a re-

---

[1] A meaning not apparent to spiritualists suggests itself. According to its original usage the word 'impress' had a meaning equivalent to that of the present-day words 'pressurize' or 'press-gang'. In a context where the circle's advancement as a whole is dependent upon the spiritual advancement of each member, where progress is thought to be communal, the relevance of the original meaning emerges.

enactment of the scene of dying. However, the symptoms are not thought to become the woman's unless the case of possession is somehow grossly mismanaged. The symptoms can be made to disappear by saying: 'Take it away, please.' Alternatively, one may cross one's arms or, less obtrusively, one's legs, in order to make one's body inaccessible to spirit influence. At one level, no doubt, such crossings may have a Christian significance. But in the case of crossing one's legs there may also be sexual undertones, in that women may bar sexual access.

The second form of possession, namely 'impression', is a slightly less spectacular procedure. This condition is thought to result when the words or thoughts of a spirit entity make themselves known to a 'sensitive'.[1] Usually such impression occurs amongst a circle of sitters. The end product is known as a 'message from spirit'. Usually such messages convey advice to some other member of the circle.

I suggest that the extreme form which spiritualism takes in many primitive societies, its necessary connection with illness, is symptomatic of a severe gap between male and female worlds. Any conflict, therefore, which arises between individuals does not find scope for mutual adjustment and manoeuvering. It involves total breakdown or illness. In our own society, by contrast, male and female spheres of activity are not as distinctly segregated; there is room for some free-play, initiative and adjustment in personal relationships. Accordingly, the relationship between the possessed and illness is conceptualized in a more oblique fashion. The woman does not herself become ill but temporarily partakes of someone else's illness. More directly, she may receive advice from spirit about her relationships with men, or advice about one of her vague collection of symptoms. These forms of possession are, therefore, consistent with and a reflection of the kind of relationship that many of these women have with men.

However, male/female relationships and the conflicts which they generate are reflected not only in acting various conditions

---

[1] Again the word 'sensitive' brings to mind associations with a photographic plate which fixes the word in the early days of photographic development.

of affliction and in messages of advice relating to the conflicts, but also in carrying out healing rituals within the circle. I referred to a significant male minority at the beginning of the chapter. The role in which men most convey this significance is that of healer. Empirically, spirit healing involves the laying on of hands by the healer to that part of the woman's body which is thought to be the cause of pain. The healer's hands lightly stroke the affected area. Frequently women will murmur: 'Oh, that's wonderful,' or, 'I can feel the power coming.' My impressions of healing are that it is a very erotic episode. The words, movements and sounds are suggestive of an ecstatic woman. Breathing is especially important; it must be slow, deep and preferably audible. In fact, this is considered a necessary part of being in contact with spirit and letting the power penetrate. If no specific part of a woman's body is given for healing it is usually the abdomen which receives attention. From the point of view of a non-spiritualist observer of this drama a few salient features emerge. These are that the interaction occurs between a man and a woman; that the man is the active partner in the interchange; that the woman is essentially passive with the exception of her expression of appreciation of the man's activities; that the interaction consists of physical contact of a decidedly non-aggressive or even tender kind.

Another significant male role consists in teaching women how to become 'receptacles' or 'instruments' of spirit. It is thought that most women are too self-controlled and inhibited to be natural 'instruments'. Hence, they must learn gradually to relax, 'to let themselves go' and submit to spirit. The man, therefore, assumes the role of a mentor. At the developing circle of which I was a member, this role is assumed by Mr Forde. Usually he is himself possessed by his male Chinese spirit-guide, Sing-Lee. In his capacity as mentor Mr Forde takes up a position immediately behind Alice's chair. Alice, whilst her mediumistic powers are highly developed as a result of the sixteen years she has sat in the circle, still has considerable difficulty in 'going under control' as opposed to becoming 'impressed' by messages or conditions. It is this 'failing' which Mr Forde tries to remedy. He very gently places both his hands on her shoulders and softly coaxes her to breathe more deeply and to relax. As Alice gradually begins to show signs of possession, as she begins to tremble and sigh, Mr Forde offers her reassurance. 'It's all right', he says, 'I'm here, I'm holding you, you're perfectly safe.' Alice, in the small, unsteady voice of the spirit possessing her, replies: 'Is it? Don't let go of me! Hold me! Hold me, won't you?' In fact, the whole drama revolves around the need to provide a safe, reassuring, male environment whilst the spirit enters. In this procedure the role of the male in guiding and touching the female is mystically sanctioned.

In both the procedures described above it seems that there is implicit in both actions and words a certain sexual element. In the first instance the woman is considered ill and, therefore, her role performance is impaired. It is this impairment which needs to be healed or put right. In the second instance the woman is thought to be inaccessible to spirit influence and unwilling to surrender her body to a spirit agency. Here the aim is to teach her to surrender her body. In both cases the agent of change is a man whose claim to give advice and help is grounded in supernatural authority.

The chapter began with the assertion that spiritualism is a response to conflict-ridden situations with men. However, conflict-reducing rituals are not sufficient evidence for this thesis. Evidence of actual conflict-ridden marriages or male female relationships must be produced. The remaining part of the chapter deals with this latter aspect.

The marital and reproductive status of members of the developing circle are represented in Figure 1. All the women members are married. However, of these, three are widowed and a further two are childless. Mrs Russell has a mentally subnormal daughter of thirty. This leaves only two women whose husbands are currently alive and whose children are not suffering from any gross abnormality. Of these two women, one, Ethel, has an outwardly stable marriage which is, how-

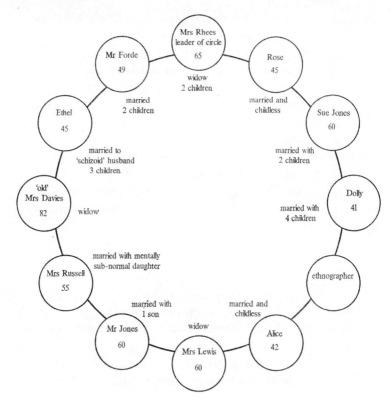

Group membership has varied slightly over the past three years.
The circle is represented in its most recent form.

Figure 1　The developing circle: marital and reproductive statuses

ever, ridden with extreme conflict. Only Dolly leads a married
life apparently free from the more obvious and spectacular
manifestations of marital disharmony.

My description of spiritual rituals as attempts at reducing
marital conflict is quite different from Robin Horton's account
of the spirit possession cult among the Kalabari. Horton (1969,
p. 38) treats the assumption of membership of a spirit possession
cult as equivalent to a 'rejection of woman's basic roles'.
Horton describes the spirits as announcing their arrival through

the appearance of some physical disability such as persistent abdominal pains or chronic limb pains. These physical ailments are thought to be remedied 'through the acceptance of marital relationships with water spirits and subsequent submission to being possessed by them' (ibid.). The first encounter with spirits, however, invariably tends to be stormy (ibid., p. 36): 'Victims seemed to agree that when it first came, it was apt to be violent, unamenable to human entreaty and unpredictable in its habits. An initial period of instruction, however, at another oru kuro woman's house, transforms it into a relatively well-disciplined, socialized being.' Horton concludes that possession by an 'oru kuro' spirit is a means whereby a woman 'transcends the sex barrier' (ibid., p. 42), in much the same way as male members of spirit possession cults are thought to transcend status barriers. According to Horton, therefore, spirit possession is not a response to childlessness or marital unhappiness. On the contrary, it is thought to create those conditions. I quote (ibid., p. 38) 'our findings accord with popular beliefs that the spirits tend to stop an oru kuro woman from having children and that such women are difficult to control, unamenable to household routine and so make bad wives.' Such, briefly, is the gist of Horton's argument. Kalabari women are supposedly reasonably married according to the marriage norms prevalent in Kalabari society but they are dissatisfied with these very norms.

The previous account of healing rituals and possession instruction in spiritualist meetings and the three following case histories of married women belonging to the circle do not suggest a relationship between the rejection of basic feminine roles and spirit possession.

Dolly is a woman whose spiritual development and marital history are closely interwoven. Dolly is a married woman in her early forties. She is Welsh, married to a wholesale dressmaker and lives in a rambling house in a well-established suburb. She is energetic, friendly and the mother of four children. Her eldest child is in early adolescence, whilst her youngest, Emma, is just three years old. This means that

Emma was conceived and born during the time that Dolly was a regular member of the circle. Though not yet myself a member of the circle at the time, the circle's attitude towards Emma's arrival has since been recounted to me. Emma was, it seems, foreseen by the circle and Dolly's pregnancy was predicted by a member of the circle, Mr Jones. This was, in fact, before Dolly had any suspicions of pregnancy herself. She claims that the child was very much an unexpected, if pleasant, surprise to her and she seems to hold the circle, at least in part, responsible for its birth. The members of the circle look upon Emma as 'a child of the circle' or as a 'spirit child'. In other words, they regard themselves as spiritual parents. However, Emma is very much a real child, unlike the spirit children which Kalabari women are supposed to bear for their spirit husbands. From the nature of the questions which Dolly receives about Emma it is quite apparent that the circle has a very real concern for her happiness and well-being.

More recently Alice has suggested that Dolly might produce another child, although the message was not very specific as to time. To date Dolly has not fulfilled this spirit prophecy by becoming pregnant. However, if and when she does conceive, another 'spirit child' will be born.

The second case-history relates to Ethel who has been an intermittent member of the circle for some eight years. Ethel is in her middle forties, married to an electrical engineer and has three adolescent children. They live in a large detached house in the suburbs of Welshtown. Ethel's marital history is a tale of endurance in the face of conflict and despair. Her husband is, according to Ethel, irresponsible with respect to money, inconsiderate towards the children and sadistic towards herself. Throughout their married life he has been involved with other women. Ethel has characterized him as an aggressive and selfish man who is utterly insensitive to the feelings of others. Apparently, he is not altogether oblivious to her opinion of him, since he eventually agreed to consult a psychiatrist at a mental hospital in Welshtown. The psychiatrist spoke to Ethel after he had seen her husband and said that there was nothing at all wrong with her but that her husband was 'schizoid'. Since this time Ethel's life has been slightly easier, for she has realized that her husband is 'a sick man', that he is suffering from an 'illness' and that it is, therefore, her duty to stick by him and to help him, even though her help may be rejected. In sum, she now regards helping her husband regain his health as her major life's task and she approaches it with fervour. Despite her stoicism, however, her situation is not a happy one.

Ethel brings to the meetings her feelings of terrible loneliness, meaninglessness and despair. These feelings find frequent expression at the meetings, both during possession and during her non-mystical states of consciousness. Thus, on one occasion, Ethel had an uncontrolled and intense fit of crying. It was not entirely clear whether she was in a state of possession or not. She turned to Mr Forde, sitting on her left, who had quite clearly 'gone' and was 'under control' by Sing-Lee. What should she do? She had 'this heaviness, pain and depression'. Should she take pills? Mr Forde said that she should not; the condition was 'mental' and pills would not remove the conflict. On hearing this Ethel was convulsed with heart-rending sobs. She screamed and cried: 'Oh my God help me!' and 'I don't want to feel alone!' Mr Jones got up and laid his hands on her shoulders. Mr Forde, still 'under control,' held her hands. The rest of us sang and prayed. All uncrossed their knees 'so as not to break the power'. In this instance, the uncrossing of knees symbolized the need to open up, or the need for co-operation and help. This was offered by all those attending with the exception of Mrs Russell, a competitive woman, who sat with her knees stubbornly crossed. She was asked why she did not help in this simple and obvious way but replied: 'Ask a silly question, get a silly answer.' Subsequently she said that she had a right to protect herself. She could not help herself let alone anyone else. She had buried her brother and her brother-in-law that very week but she did not bring the condition with her to the circle. In other words, Mrs Russell was envious of the attention and healing power which Ethel was getting and which she was not.

In Ethel's case, however, there does not seem to be any turning away from her husband. In her seemingly endless discussions with me she has emphasized the impossibility of leaving her husband, both from the practical and the moral point of view. Ethel's loyalty persists, despite the fact that her husband is, to all appearances, a man incapable of fulfilling the normal duties of a husband. This is a situation which does not admit of an easy practical solution, even with the help of spirit. Ethel is, however, given reassurance and comfort, especially from the two male members of the circle, Mr Forde and Mr Jones.

According to Ethel herself the initial, causal factor in her association with spiritualism was the fact that she is married to 'an ambitious and power hungry man'. This caused her a great deal of suffering. However, through spiritualism she realized that a different kind of life was possible. She says that she hopes to learn more about herself and about 'life' through spiritualism.

A final case-history is provided by Alice, already introduced in an earlier chapter. She is forty-two and childless and her husband, Selwyn, is forty-four. They live in an old semi-detached house on the outskirts of Welshtown which is, in fact, the area which Selwyn covers in his work as an insurance agent. Alice was twenty-five when she married Selwyn, which means that they have now been married for seventeen years. She has been a member of the developing circle for sixteen years. According to gossip, Alice had a daughter who died in infancy, although she has never directly spoken of this to me.

Alice has told me many times that her husband is 'a very good man'; also, that her relationship with him is a very satisfactory and happy one. However, the events on a journey to London with both of them and my frequent visits to their home do not altogether support this claim. In terms of character Alice and Selwyn are different. Alice is a gaunt, tired-looking woman for whom the processes of day-to-day living seem to present constant and exorbitant demands upon her inner resources. In contrast to her worn apperance she has an unexpectedly loud and high-pitched laugh. Selwyn, on the other hand, is plump with an easy-going and comfortable outlook. Not surprisingly their communication lacks directness. Their interaction seems to consist of a series of mutual taunts. This was made clear on the journey to London. The entire time was taken up with argument. Both Selwyn and Alice tried to prove that his and her contribution to the marriage respectively was greater and involved greater sacrifice and effort and each appealed to me to act as witness to and judge of their claim. However, there was another theme woven into Alice's side of the argument. She seemed to suggest that she could lead a marvellously independent and carefree existence without Selwyn. She could go to London, buy new clothes, get a new man and so on. Selwyn's response to this line of argument was a mixture of scorn and indignation. Having exhausted this line of attack, Alice adopted less sophisticated tactics. 'You're stupid', she said. To which Selwyn replied: 'You must be out of your tiny little mind', and then (aside to me): 'She wakes me at four o'clock in the morning and says "talk to me" and now she says I'm stupid!'

The importance which Alice attaches to independence is understandable in view of the differences between her and Selwyn's background. Alice was born in Welshtown in the house in which she now lives and has spent all her life there. Selwyn was born in Aberport. However, he lived in London for over a year and was in the RAF for some years, during which time he was stationed in the Far East as well as travelling a good deal. He says: 'I did my living before I married.' Selwyn's experience of life is, therefore, altogether a more varied and sophisticated one. This discrepancy in their backgrounds and experience seems to constitute a source of friction between them. Moreover, since Alice is childless she enjoys few of the traditional rewards of the married woman. Nevertheless, it must be emphasized that Alice considers herself happily married and, more important still, that she describes Selwyn as being very understanding and considerate. She could not want a better partner, she says. This would suggest the conclusion that their conflicts are not entirely due to interpersonal friction but are generated by the norms and rewards governing the behaviour of a married woman in Welshtown. However, the distinction between simple inter-personal hostility and institutionalized sex role conflict is impossible to maintain at any level other than a purely theoretical one.

These three case-histories are sufficiently apposite to suggest that an alternative to the anthropologists' thesis of rejection of feminine roles may be possible. Both Ethel's and Alice's histories are of conflict with their husbands where an alternative is nevertheless not envisaged. Dolly's marriage receives constant spiritual support and encouragement from the circle.

Further, the response to the arrival of a new male member may also be relevant to the theme of this chapter. Mr Forde began attending meetings at the end of March 1970, at Mrs Rhees's suggestion. However, since he works 'shifts' he is unable to attend every third meeting. Very little seems to be known of his background by other members of the circle. In a sense, I know more about his spirit-guide, Sing-Lee, than about Mr Forde himself. It is known that he has been a medium for many years and does occasional 'platform-work'. He is married and the messages which he receives from spirit suggest that his marriage is not an altogether happy one. Otherwise information is largely restricted to his physical appearance. He is a small man with a neat moustache. He is in his late forties, usually very quiet and retiring with the exception of the times when he is 'under control'. At such times he speaks loudly and confidently. Mr Forde's mediumistic powers are, in fact, highly developed. His possession states are always of long duration, usually lasting the entire meeting. Mr Forde is usually possessed by one of two spirits. They are his spirit-guides. The first is Sing-Lee, a Chinaman previously mentioned, the other is a Welsh preacher. Both appear to be well-read, especially in religious writings. This accounts perhaps in part for the immediate welcome with which Mr Forde's arrival was greeted. He was described as 'wonderful' and in the opening prayer Mrs

Rhees asked that 'our brother' should be visited by Sing-Lee. Whilst Mr Forde is in a state of possession Mrs Rhees says: 'We love you to come and we hope you will come again.' The meetings are almost entirely dominated by Mr Forde since his arrival. If any member of the circle turns to Mrs Rhees with a query she replies rather apologetically that she is ignorant and refers the query to Mr Forde. This deferential behaviour is in marked contrast to her previous role prior to Mr Forde's advent. Even Mr Jones has become imbued with this deference to the extent that he has ceased his healing activities on the evenings when Mr Forde is present, for fear of impeding Mr Forde's possession activities. Mrs Rhees, however, reminded Mr Jones that his services were very much missed after which he quietly resumed his gentle healing round. The description of the welcome extended to Mr Forde thus goes against the notion that men are peripheral to spiritualism.

Perhaps the activities of the circle provide an illustration of what Gluckman (1956, p. 109) may have meant by 'licence in ritual'. However, in the case of the developing circle, the ritual is not merely a safety valve, as Gluckman seems to imply, but a positive attempt at understanding and reconciliation. Gluckman is interested in that aspect of ritual which is devoted to the 'acting out' of conflicts, hence, his interest in 'rites of reversal'. Gluckman describes these rites in the following way (ibid.): 'These rites of reversal obviously include a protest against the established order; and in many rituals their performance is believed to achieve success and prosperity for the group which practises them.' Later Gluckman cites several cases of women participating in rituals involving 'obscene and domineering acts' (ibid.). However, Gluckman describes these rituals as being 'statements of rebellion not of revolution' (ibid., p. 122), and as the 'licensed statement of conflict' (ibid., p. 134). In other words, Gluckman's prior assumption is that there is an overall acceptance of the social order and that the rituals of conflict are merely an airing of frustrations, which make subsequent submission to and acceptance of the social order seem less constraining. Specifically rituals involving

Zulu women are an outlet for grievances and frustrations felt with regard to men and a simultaneous insurance of women's continued subservience to men.

In Welshtown there seems to be a similar overall acceptance of the social order and woman's place in it. This acceptance is apparent from the way in which women speak of their husbands, their own roles within marriage and the institution of marriage itself. However, not only is the notion of revolution inapplicable to spiritualism, the notion of a ritual of rebellion is equally foreign to the spiritualist outlook. Possession behaviour does not involve a reversal of sex roles as described in the Shango cult in Trinidad (Mischel and Mischel, 1958, p. 256). On the contrary, spiritualists are usually possessed by spirits of their own sex and during possession men and women embody in their behaviour those attributes considered to be ideally masculine and feminine respectively.

Spiritualist ritual may involve the 'acting out' of conflicts, but this is clearly related to an attempt to understand and resolve marital difficulties. However, whether these difficulties stem from interpersonal hostility or from the frustrations associated with the traditional feminine role is difficult to establish. In practice, the two are inextricably interwoven. However, ritual is not only concerned with conflict. Spiritualist healing ritual is a symbolic expression of male and female roles ideally conceived. Although in everyday life men and women may fall short of these ideals, in ritual the strength of these ideals is reaffirmed.

I hope this chapter will have contributed towards elucidating a remark of the nineteenth-century idealist philosopher, Francis Herbert Bradley (1930, p. 66): 'When men say that possession is the grave of love I am reminded that a religion may begin with the resurrection.' Whether or not Bradley discovered a truth about the human heart, his statement is certainly of value as a contribution towards the understanding of the social anthropology of religion.

Chapter 5   Church and circle

This chapter is about competition and conflict between individuals and between groups. It is concerned with the undercurrents which disturb the otherwise ordinarily peaceful encounters with spirit. On the one hand, spiritualists are involved in a search for personal salvation; whilst on the other hand, they find that encounters with spirit offer and tempt towards a search for personal power. The search for personal salvation is community orientated and constructive. All members benefit from the spiritual progress of one member and such progress is thought to be indicative of good interpersonal rapport. On the other hand, the search for individual power is thought to be destructive of the good of the group and a perversion of the aims of true communication with spirit.

Underlying this discussion are two assumptions. First, the fierceness of competition and conflict is determined in part by the level of commitment to spiritualism. If a person sees rewards as coming solely from within a spiritualist context, then his battles within that field will be that much fiercer. Second, conflict is endemic to spiritualist ideology. One of the attractions of spiritualism is that it deceptively promises high ritual status to all adherents: spiritualist doctrine recognizes the universality of mediumistic or spiritual power in a latent, if not manifest form. Moreover, mediumistic power is the currency in terms of which status within the movement is acquired. However, high status is by definition scarce; if it is too easily acquired it loses value and thus destroys itself. Thus there is conflict and the elements of self-destruction at the very core of spiritualist doctrine. As a result, whilst the theoretical universality of mediumistic power is readily acknowledged, its actual manifestations constitute a threat to all committed spiritualists. This threat is increased by the absence of clearly formulated beliefs and structure within the groups. This disruptive potential of personal revelations is well described by Charles Glock and Rodney Stark (1965, p. 57):

> whenever a mystic or monk or devout believer engages
> in a meditation or interpretation of the scriptures he can
> create a new creed. This possibility poses a constant threat
> of cleavage within the group. . . . But despite these
> controls and many other mechanisms which have been
> employed to preclude or channel revelationary activity
> men continue to return from their encounters with
> divinity with new and heretical versions of 'eternal truth'.

This conflict is reflected in the formation of what, in the classroom context, Colin Lacey (1970, p. 85) terms 'group norms' and 'anti-group norms'. Competition for status leads to the alternating operation of these two sets of norms. Both sets of norms can be and are operated by the same person in different contexts. Group norms operate where status is safe; anti-group norms operate where status is threatened. Group norms involve the ready acceptance of all messages; they involve a willingness to sympathize with other spiritualists, to refrain from unnecessarily harsh criticism and a readiness to give and to receive advice from other circle members. In short, group norms involve a readiness to abide by the explicit and implicit rules of the group thereby expressing solidarity.

By contrast, anti-group norms involve the rejection of messages given by other circle members. They cast doubt on the genuineness of mediumistic performance; there is criticism of the mediumistic performance as well as of the sincerity of the medium. Unethical and base motives are attributed to the person assuming a mediumistic role. Anti-group norms involve the violation of the explicit and implicit rules of the group.

Competition for status exists not only between individual group members, but also between circles and between churches and circles. The relationship between church and circle is an ambivalent one. On the one hand, the circle is dependent upon the church in that it ultimately expects recognition from the larger organizations. On the other hand, the circle acts rather like a self-appointed and stringent conscience of the church. The church and the leading mediums associated with the church have established reputations. However, from the standpoint of circle members the high ritual status of church mediums is an obstacle to the easy spiritual progress of the circle. From the point of view of the church the circle and its activities are a necessary, if threatening, development. The result of this relationship is that the church regards the circle with mixed feelings of envy and disparagement whilst the circles express feelings of moral outrage at church activities as well as secret satisfaction at the fear which their own activities are evoking.

The nature of competition, the way in which alternating sets of norms are manipulated and the ideological idiom in which conflict is expressed are best illustrated by a series of examples of conflict situations.

Conflict between individuals

Mrs Russell
Spiritualist meetings often include one person who embodies the antithesis of all spiritualist values. Mrs Russell, a member of the developing circle, is one such person. She consistently breaks all the spiritualist rules governing behaviour at meetings. Her rule-breaking is inevitably a target for criticism from other circle members. Her conversation is thought to be 'material'. She corrects other people's messages from spirit. Thus, if Mrs Rhees gives a symbolic object to one of the other circle members, say, a bunch of deep-red flowers, Mrs Russell will correct the message by saying that the flowers are not really deep-red, 'but more of a coral colour'. Mrs Russell

corrects messages throughout every meeting, even though in theory two spiritualists are thought not to be able to receive the same message at the same time. However, this is a theoretical issue which is a point of debate among spiritualists. Messages which Mrs Russell herself claims to receive from spirit, she does not 'give out' but keeps to herself. Thus, during the course of a meeting, whilst others are exchanging messages, Mrs Russell rocks backwards and forwards muttering to herself: 'Thank you, thank you, that's wonderful'. Afterwards Alice asks me: 'Do you think she's getting anything? I don't think she's getting anything. If it's so bloody wonderful why doesn't she bloody well give it out?' Mrs Russell also sits with her legs crossed although she knows that this is against spiritualist custom and that in doing so she is refusing to participate and is obstructing the joint spiritual endeavours of the group. However, despite the fact that Mrs Russell has been a 'loner' and a constant target for criticism and resentment for many years, she has nevertheless not been evicted from the circle. This is partly because the ethos of meetings is such as to demand tolerance. In greater part, however, her presence which embodies all the anti-group norms provides a focus for the definition or reassertion of values. In a context where there is little formal opportunity for the expression of spiritualist values, opposition and conflict may have a sustaining effect on the spiritualist ethos. Perhaps Mrs Russell found that she did not win when she played the game according to the accepted spiritualist rules. Some success was only achieved by totally abandoning them.

Mrs Rhees and Mr O'Keefe
Some years before my admission to the developing circle acute conflict developed between Mrs Rhees, the leader of the circle, and Mr O'Keefe, a medium of long-standing and highly developed powers. As a result of this conflict Mr O'Keefe left the circle and severed his relationship with spiritualism in general. The dispute between them was not

ostensibly related to competition for ritual status, but was an ideological one derived from incompatible views about the role of the circle in relation to the spirit world. Mr O'Keefe was of the opinion that the spirits should be taught to come 'properly'; each sitter's 'gatekeeper' should ensure that the spirits did not bring unruly or improper conditions with them. Otherwise, adulterers, murderers and perverts could, he thought, return to the circle. Mrs Rhees, on the other hand, thought that all spirits should be encouraged to return to the circle and to 'bring their condition with them'. According to Mrs Rhees this is the only way in which spirits can be helped to overcome their condition and be freed from their earthly circumstances. In this conflict situation Mrs Rhees triumphed, with the result that Mr O'Keefe, who may have aspired to leadership of the circle, departed.

Thus it could be said that the therapeutic element in the circle's activities had triumphed over the didactic element. However, Mrs Rhees continues to be criticized on the grounds that she does not exercise sufficiently strict censorship. It was seemingly her sensitivity to such criticism which prompted her to suspend Ethel from the circle a few years back. Ethel has been a member of the circle for eight years with the exception of a year's requested absence. Ethel accounts for this absence in terms of 'a severe emotional shock' as a result of which she was thought to constitute a disturbing influence on the circle.

In Ethel's case the circle felt that its therapeutic powers were being overtaxed. Thus whilst the circle sees itself as being supportive and helping its members to manage problems, it nevertheless recognizes that certain problems are beyond the scope of the circle and that the individual will benefit little from circle membership. At least, if members with such problems do get benefit, they may do so at the expense of other circle members.

Conflict between groups
Competition between individuals for the acquisition of spiritual rewards is reflected in relationships between groups. Conflict is

expressed in the mutual criticism exchanged between the developing circle and other spiritualist churches. On average, between half-an-hour and an hour is devoted each week to general conversation in the course of which other groups and mediums are fiercely criticized. Usually the criticism is expressed as disapproval of the alleged self-interest permeating the performance of other mediums. Members of the circle claim that other mediums are not at all concerned with service or communication with spirit. Instead, so the criticism goes, they are anxious to establish their own personal reputations and further their own personal ends. In Alice's words, they are concerned with: 'I, I, I and not spirit.' For that very reason their messages are 'material' and cite trivial facts and figures in an effort to establish their ritual authenticity. However, according to circle members, although they may produce a more immediate satisfaction in their recipient, they cannot be of lasting value. Mrs Rhees is especially firm in pointing out that her messages are 'higher' than those of other mediums.

In return the feelings of other spiritualists towards the developing circle are not altogether kind. This is partly because competition for admission to the circle is very keen and those who are admitted are regarded with considerable envy. However, this envy is soon transmuted into hostile criticism. The general attitude towards the circle is illustrated by Alice's encounter with Mrs Cavendish, a well-known and spectacular medium. Alice decided to go to Mrs Cavendish in order to receive healing for a cyst in the left eye. The cyst was extremely painful, but as it was not malignant the doctor had advised that it should not be removed. The cyst was a constant course of anxiety and pain to Alice and in despair Alice decided to turn to Mrs Cavendish for help. Mrs Cavendish has a home circle, which meets weekly at her house. As a result her reputation is high. Consequently, Alice's expectations of the meeting were also high, in part also because Mrs Cavendish had been a life-long friend of Alice's mother. The meeting between Alice and Mrs Cavendish had been arranged by Ethel as writing or telephoning had seemed difficult to Alice. Alice had been led to believe that there would be only one other person there. Instead she found thirteen others. Under such circumstances she thought that healing could not possibly be successful. So the encounter started off on the wrong foot. Furthermore, when Mrs Cavendish gave Alice a message she said that all the elements around Alice were 'Wrong! Wrong! Wrong!' The people around Alice were also said to exert a destructive influence on Alice. Whatever the intention of the message, Alice immediately judged that Mrs Cavendish was referring to the developing circle. At this point Alice was 'boiling inside' and had difficulty in restraining herself from leaving or screaming aloud. When Mrs Cavendish placed her hands on Alice, she had difficulty in keeping still since Mrs Cavendish's touch had now become so loathsome to her. When she eventually got home she had not been able to speak to Selwyn because had she done so he would have forbidden her to have anything more to do with spiritualism. So Alice had retired silently to bed knowing that if Wednesday nights were taken away from her, life would seem empty and not worth living.

Alice's very plausible interpretation of this meeting was that Mrs Cavendish was jealous of her alliance with the developing circle. Other members of the circle to whom this incident was recounted immediately agreed with this way of construing the situation. They admitted that Mrs Cavendish could be a very good speaker and still suffer from such personal failings as pride and arrogance. It was stressed that the failings of particular mediums, which sometimes influenced the messages they gave, did not detract from the validity of spiritualism as such. All rallied to support Alice at this moment of distress. Mrs Rhees said that Mrs Cavendish had not been speaking as a 'true' spiritualist. It was the business of all messages to help elevate the thoughts. Instead, Alice had been 'cast down' by Mrs Cavendish. Mrs Russell described the situation by saying that Alice had gone for help but had been rejected and scorned instead. Feeling more secure in the midst of this wealth of sympathy, Alice disclosed that Mrs Cavendish had said Alice had 'three times lost her mind'. This again was treated as a shocking and unethical thing to say. How could she have lost her mind, Alice asked, if she knew what she was doing? Alice knew her nerves were bad but Mrs Cavendish had gone a little too far. And, what was more, the lack of success of healing and the persistence of her cyst did not make her nerves any better.

King Street
Another conflict-ridden area is the relationship between the church in Park Street and that in King Street. In this drama the leading roles are played by Mrs Daimler and Miss Ryecroft of Park Street and Mrs Joseph and Miss Lantern of King Street. Considerable rivalry and bad feeling exists between each of the women mentioned. This finds expression in accusations which doubt the genuineness of mediumship, impute an excess of greed and ambition to the medium and sometimes suggest dishonesty with respect to church funds. Such criticism is usually voiced and subsequently repeated among members of one church or circle. There is, however, sufficient overlapping of membership for this criticism to reach the church against which it is directed.

One instance of a conflict situation is provided by the sequence of events following on from Mrs Jones's death. Mrs Jones was the president of King Street until her death in April 1969. The aftermath of her sudden and unexpected death produced feelings of dismay, uncertainty and helplessness. There being no one to conduct services, that is, to announce hymns and say introductory prayers, this role was temporarily filled by Miss Lantern. After about two weeks, however, it was decided that Mrs Joseph was to be the new president of King Street. Subsequently, however, Mrs Joseph proved to be an unwise choice of leader. Mrs Joseph is in her late fifties. She is a cripple and walks with a very pronounced limp. Having been a widow for many years she met Mr Joseph at the developing circle a few years ago. Shortly afterwards the two were married at one of the few spiritualist wedding ceremonies,

but, her second marriage, too, ended abruptly in further
widowhood after only a year. Widowhood and physical handi-
cap are, however, the least of her disadvantages as far as
spiritualism is concerned. Mrs Joseph is a gauche woman.
More important than her physical awkwardness are her social
defects and slowness. Not surprisingly, she shows a marked
lack of mediumistic talent. Although not generally acknowledged as such, she leaves the impression of being at least
partially deaf. Her own voice is correspondingly raised and
strident. In view of these many shortcomings and her lack of
perception, her choice as president seems a mysterious one.
More interesting yet are the subsequent varying responses to
Mrs Joseph's leadership. Criticism of Mrs Joseph as leader and
medium was plentiful. She was said to be motivated by personal
ambition rather than the desire to communicate the intimations
of spirit. Indeed, her unpopularity was such that numbers soon
dropped to half of what they had previously been. On Thursday
afternoons numbers were sometimes as low as six or seven.
During this period of transition and crisis Mrs Daimler and
Miss Ryecroft rallied to the support of King Street. Mrs
Daimler and Miss Ryecroft came to all the meetings which did
not clash with services in Park Street. Frequently, Mr Daimler
was brought along to play the organ.

Mrs Joseph's term of leadership lasted barely a year, for in
June 1970, she died without warning following a diabetic
coma. Concern for the future of King Street was widespread
and increasing. 'Whatever her faults' Mrs Joseph had been 'a
good spiritualist'.

After a brief period of closure King Street re-opened with
Miss Lantern as president. Miss Lantern is about seventy. She
is very infirm with a weak heart and severe rheumatoid
arthritis. Ordinarily, she has a pleasant manner, being quiet,
kindly and concerned. On occasions, however, she has shown
herself to have a loud and acid tongue. Although in many
respects Miss Lantern made a good president anxieties about
King Street persisted. It was generally agreed that Miss Lantern
was too old and too weak to be able to fill the leadership role

adequately. These anxieties were given a real basis when, after a few months, Miss Lantern suffered a stroke. One half of her body was found to be paralysed and chances of recovery were thought to be small. Many attributed her illness to the increased strain and responsibility which presidency had brought with it.

Following Miss Lantern's forced retirement King Street was closed and no further services were held there. Soon afterwards an announcement appeared in the local paper informing its readers that King Street was closed for an indefinite period. No reasons were given. Subsequent conversation with spiritualists revealed the true extent of the chaos in King Street. There appeared to be no one in King Street willing or able to act as successor to Miss Lantern. Furthermore, King Street was lacking in any decision-making procedures whereby such a person could be selected. Finally, such attempts would have been physically obstructed by the fact that Miss Lantern had taken the key of King Street with her to hospital and refused to give it up. Despite the reactions of shock, shame and horrified disapproval which Miss Lantern's behaviour aroused, no effective counter-action was taken. The situation was, however, the subject of prolonged discussion. Members of the circle considered various ways of literally and metaphorically forcing Miss Lantern's hand and obtaining the key of King Street. Also considered was the question of a possible successor to Miss Lantern. The situation remained unsolved for almost half a year. The church was, however, eventually re-opened.

The sequel of this history is an illustration of the theme of continuity and change. It reports my findings after a term's absence from field-work. The account of new developments lends support to the main structural features outlined earlier.

The circle is unchanged and meets regularly as before. The most significant development is that members of the circle have re-opened King Street. An advertisement was again put in the local paper this time announcing that there was to be a meeting to which everyone interested in the future of King Street was invited. At the meeting it was decided that Mr Forde was to be the new president, Dolly was to be the secretary and Ethel was to be the treasurer. Thus there was a virtual take-over bid by the circle of King Street. However, dissension is already rife, chiefly around Ethel. For example, Alice claims that Ethel is keeping many people away from King Street by her domineering and outspoken ways. However, not only is her manner unacceptable but she is unable to contain her personal problems. Ethel's husband has now left her and her sixteen-year-old daughter is expecting a child. Not unnaturally, Ethel treats each meeting as an opportunity to air her sorrows and anxieties. This persistent and unrelenting search for help vexes others.

This assumption of leadership roles is interesting in terms of the light which it casts on previous circle activities. Retrospectively the circle can be seen to have provided a training ground for spiritualist mediums or leaders. This is especially true of Dolly who was given endless encouragement to 'let spirit take over'. The progress made by circle members is apparent in all. However, it is especially noticeable in Mr Forde. He has assumed a more youthful and urbane look. He has grown sideboards and his hair is smoothly slicked forward across his forehead. He has acquired a pair of gold-rimmed spectacles and a silk knitted tie. In sum he has the serene and competent look of the successful professional. The others, also, have an air of buoyancy. The circle has fulfilled its expectations and sees itself as progressing towards greater things.

At the first meeting I attended after a term's absence, Mr Forde was as usual possessed first by the spirit of a Welsh preacher and then by Sing-Lee. The Welsh preacher gave no healing but delivered a sermon on the art of spirit mediumship. Sing-Lee was less authoritarian and more informal in his approach. He began by giving spirit healing to all members of the circle. Then he engaged in a dialogue during which those with queries were instructed and enlightened. Dolly asked him what should be done if the words received from spirit caused dissension. Sing-Lee replied: 'Let the words come out as

bitter as gall, yet they will be received with gratitude and love.'
Dolly voiced another problem. Often she felt the presence of
spirit and knew it wanted to communicate through her, yet
she was afraid that the words which she gave out would be
from her own head and not from spirit. Because of this fear
she held back without saying anything and thus did not give
spirit a chance to communicate. Sing-Lee suggested that
when she felt the presence of spirit, yet was unable to give forth
the words of spirit, she should begin by saying a prayer or
psalm and then she would find that spirit would take over.

Before leaving, Sing-Lee warned everyone not to forget that
there was a tiger lurking around the circle. Spiritual advancement has its drawbacks as well as its rewards. In this case, the
circle's increasing spiritual powers were attracting more
attention from the spirit world. The circle's visibility was thus
increasing. This visibility brought with it dangers, for with
advancement, the circle's vulnerability to evil spirits increased.
It was more than ever important not to sit alone for fear of
the lurking spirit tiger.

This warning was couched in religious language. However,
the dangers to which it refers and the emphasis on solidarity
are readily applicable to the precariousness and isolation
associated with any position of leadership whether secular or
mystical.

This account of succession seems to be typical of spiritualism.
It is apparent that the process of leadership emergence is
haphazard and lacking in any structure or form. In the
absence of co-ordinated and effective opposition an aspiring
leader will make what amounts to almost a private decision to
assume leadership. In such times of crisis personal and group
animosity is overcome and solidarity is shown. Women who
consider each other rivals in one situation, will support each
other where the continued survival of a spiritualist church is at
stake.

A distinction needs to be made, however, between formal
administrative leadership and mystical leadership. Whilst
spiritualists are conspicuously unable to produce leaders of

the former category there is no lack of aspirants to mystical leadership. In a sense all spiritualists are trained for leadership through the encouragement to develop their mediumistic powers. Once these traits are developed, however, it is discovered to one's disappointment that they do not automatically qualify for leadership, since the market is already flooded. Spiritualism provides many examples of mediums who could be said to have fallen into disuse.

Hollander's analysis of leadership helps to make intelligible the processes of acquiring mediumistic recognition. Hollander (1964, p. 16) says: 'leader denotes an individual with a status that permits him to exercise influence over certain other individuals. Specifically, our concern is directed towards leaders deriving status from followers who may accord or withdraw it, in an essentially free interchange within a group context.' And of status he says (ibid., p. 17): 'To say that an individual has status does not describe an attribute or a stable pattern of his behaviour; rather it describes the relationship of that individual to certain others and their attendant behaviour towards him. Interpersonal perception is a necessary part of this process.' Hollander's analysis of leadership in terms of function and context rather than intrinsic leadership traits fits in very well with the spiritualist concept of 'power', where qualities of mystical leadership are defined in terms of the central activities of the group. Furthermore, status as a medium is conferred by the opinions of other spiritualists. Invitations to take services and to act as mediums are the result of acknowledgment by other church members.

Hollander's analysis of leadership helps to expose a contradiction, already noted, intrinsic to spiritualist theory. This acknowledges the universality of mediumistic talent and its status-conferring powers. At the same time status and acknowledged leadership must by definition be scarce; otherwise, they would no longer be what they are. Competition for ownership of true doctrine from spirit will, therefore, always be competition for scarce resources. Thus there is an inherent conflict in spiritualist beliefs. Attitudes towards developing mediums and circles are always ambivalent and contradictory.

The situation is one which promotes conflict and hostility. However, there are also a number of checks on competition. One is the belief, already referred to, that no two mediums can receive the same message from spirit. Theoretically, this tenet should eliminate situations where one medium corrects or improves upon the messages received by another medium. In practice, however, this device is not always effective. Another belief aimed to subdue competition relates to the shared benefits thought to result from mediumistic development. It is thought that the spiritual development of one member of the group elevates the spiritual tone of the entire group. Rivalry is less likely where such beliefs are held. Despite these institutionalized checks competition appears endemic to the spiritualist movement.

Spiritualism has been presented as one among a limited number of coping techniques open to women with a traditional feminine role. It is an example of the way in which ritual is used to accommodate oneself to such a role. Concepts of illness and health provide a recurring ingredient of these ritual beliefs and behaviour; preoccupations with bodily ailments provide the symbolic idiom in which statements about social relationships are made. Thus ideals of friendship, sympathy and co-operation are offered within the circle as models for relationships elsewhere. However, no attempts to solve problems by dramatically altering the situation which gives rise to them are made. Instead, there is an attempt throughout to provide a number of symbolic equivalents of the stressful or difficult situation.

The advice-seeking aspects of spirit possession have been noticed by psychiatrists. For example, M. G. Field (1960) focuses attention on the advice-giving role of mediums and oracles in Ghana. However, this aspect of spirit possession has to some extent been neglected by social anthropologists. Current approaches to spirit possession interpret it as a response to undesirable situations which are thereby remedied. In other words, spirit possession is attributed a direct and functional significance. This chapter shows that the link between spirit possession and the antecedent conditions, which it is designed to remedy, need not be as direct and unmediated as current theories suggest. I argue that the advice-seeking aspect of spiritualism consists of the need to provide relevant explanations

and symbols for problems which range from the interpersonal and emotional to the medical. Thus spiritualism does
not resolve problem situations by bestowing attention or status
where otherwise these would not be available. Rather, through
spiritualism, problems are defined and thereby understood and
managed.

However, an attenuated sense in which spiritualism may be
seen as linking previous problem situations with subsequent
privileges is in respect of time. Most messages from spirit
make some reference to a specific point in time in the future.
Whether the messages give advice about personal problems,
practical affairs or health matters, nearly all refer to points
in time. For example, when illness is the subject of a message, a
diagnosis is rarely given without a prognosis. In this sense, the
medium has control over time since he or she sees past events
as clearly as future ones.

However, the acquisition of power and prestige, otherwise
denied, is not the chief motivating force in becoming a spiritualist. Striving for prestige and authority is incidental to the
central goals of spiritualism. These involve an active and
creative response on the part of their holders.

In a previous chapter the privacy associated with the experience of pain was brought out. The need for definitions and
explanations is related to this experience of privacy. John
Berger (1967, p. 75) says of illness: 'To have a complaint
recognized, that is to say, defined, limited and depersonalized
is to be made stronger. Any example offers hope. But the
conviction of being unique destroys all examples.' In this
chapter I do not examine the uniqueness or privacy of the
experience of pain, but rather the provision of examples. (The
sense of uniqueness creates the demand that the illness be seen
as part of a more general pattern, that it be seen as one instance
of a recurring series of events; that is, that it be defined and be
given a symbolic meaning.)

The emphasis on definitions and explanations is particularly
strong in developing circles. Among other things, developing
mediums are instructed in how to present messages from spirit.

Before the meetings are officially opened there is usually between half-an-hour and an hour of general conversation. Much of this conversation is devoted to a detailed discussion of the ailments of members and their friends. Suggestions of diagnoses, remedies, preventive measures, analyses of causes and prognoses are made. A characteristic of these conversations is that each remark, however trivial it may seem to me, is treated seriously and given due consideration. No one is ignored.

Rose, for example, has a long history of illness. During her five years' attendance at spiritualist meetings she has suffered from ulcers in the stomach and intestines, and more recently, from stones in the right kidney. These received an independent diagnosis at a local hospital. Although it had been generally acknowledged that Rose was in need of help and advice the gravity of her situation was not fully realized. However, after one particular meeting Rose made the following dramatic announcement: 'I may as well tell you all now that I'm to go into hospital to have my right kidney removed.' After the initial period of shocked silence advice flowed from all sides. Alice was immediately possessed by a spirit that screamed: 'Don't do it, don't do it!' Mrs Lewis, by contrast, seemed to think that such advice was against the law. Mrs Russell insisted that a distinction could be drawn between stones and gravel, and claimed spiritual authority for her insistence that Rose had gravel and not stones. There followed a general discussion on the difference between stones and gravel. Alternative courses of action were considered: the advisability of having another X-ray, an exploratory operation and so on. Rose herself said that she had received so much help from her spirit friends that she could not expect them to be concerned with her problems all the time. Indeed, although she had once suffered from ulcers they had completely disappeared as a result of spirit healing.

In contrast to the series of practical suggestions that Rose is offered before the actual commencement of the service, is the role that Rose is allowed to play during the service itself. She is permitted, although at the expense of considerable criticism from the others, to become possessed by very distressed spirits. She curls up into a foetal posture, clings to Mrs Rhees's hand (her position in the circle is a strategic one) and whimpers. She whispers in a pathetic infant's voice as one abandoned in the snow to die. Alternatively, she is a child who has lost its 'mummy and daddy and brothers and sisters'.

Frequently Mrs Rhees talks specifically about the defining and symbolizing the activities of the circle. She encourages with the words: 'Keep your thoughts high, keep them pure!' She disapproves of the way in which most mediums work by 'reeling off lists of names' and describing 'material conditions' as opposed to spiritual ones. By spirituality, Mrs Rhees is referring to symbolism. A symbolic message is one which the recipient has to work on and to unravel, there being no one-to-one relationship between the message and reality. In other words, an active response involving interpretation and re-assessment of one's condition is demanded. This preoccupation with symbolizing and defining activities suggests a certain similarity with 'consciousness-raising' sessions of Women's Lib. groups, although I do not wish to press the analogy too far. Mrs Rhees has described her interest in symbolism as an interest in picture language. Recently she came across the word 'hieroglyphs' in an encyclopaedia. She looked it up in a dictionary and found that it meant 'picture language'. At last she could put a name to her passion!

An interesting similarity emerges here with L. E. Ucko's work on the relationship between children's play patterns and stress experiences (1967). Ucko provided her children with a variety of toy bricks representing various objects such as trees, houses and animals, She then found that children could be put into one of two categories, according to whether they used the toy bricks to construct a 'rigid' or 'normal' world. Ucko characterizes the 'rigid world' as one in which there is an uneven use of the play space, where toy bricks are arranged in strict lines or clumps and where there is little mixing of types of bricks. The 'N-world' by contrast is characterized by an even use of space and little attempt at geometrical organization. It is a display of creative chaos. It seems that there is a similarity here between the kind of symbolic messages that mediums are taught to give and the construction of N-worlds. Both are characterized by the absence of a rigid patterning of reality. Both word symbols and toy patterns should be susceptible of numerous interpretations which the observer or hearer can select according to his inclination.

Examples of messages from spirit referring to situations of pain and suffering could be multiplied endlessly. However, it may suffice to give a few illustrations of messages received in King Street. Mr Hornby is speaking in King Street one evening in the summer of 1969. He is at a desk surrounded by a circle of thirty ageing women, all seated. He is a slow-speaking sad-looking man. He appears dignified, always fully in control of himself and is spoken of with respect by spiritualists. He is 'a lovely gentleman'.

He is addressing an overweight woman in her late fifties, who stares at the floor: 'You know it's not easy. I don't know what is here, but there's something here that ties my hands together. I don't know whether it's your condition, or someone that's near you or around you, on the material. But I want to say it will be removed. I feel tired. I feel my eyes are tired. I feel my eyes are aching. I feel more or less on my own. It's your condition? You understand?' 'Yes' (very softly). 'And as I'm getting it, I'm getting a message from mother to you: "Don't worry, dear; we will watch over you. Whatever help you want, you will be able to obtain wherever you go." And with the mother's love, I feel they are protecting you all the way.'

Another message at the same meeting is given to a tall gaunt woman in her sixties: 'And you see, you are our concern tonight. And they're coming back ..., I don't know. ... Do you feel, at the present time, that you're on a crossroads? And you'd like an answer tonight: shall I go right or shall I go left or shall I go straight on? That has been your thought tonight. Where is the break and where is the turning? Why? ... Let me tell you, dear: be patient a little. There is a path being made in front of you. There will be no turning. It will be a straight road. But on that road you will find more sunshine than you have had during the last years.'

Finally, a message to a woman around forty: 'I am getting a terrific feeling at the top of my head. Do you get that pain? Do you suffer from headaches? And would there be someone that went on that suffered in the same way too? I feel all the pressure is at the top of the head.' 'Yes.' 'Who is this, dear? I want to say, just rest and give them a thought.'

In expounding the nature of spiritualism, Sing-Lee, Mr Forde's spirit-guide, has said: 'You are not dealing with something that is logic. You are dealing with something that is beautiful. That is like the gossamer wing of a butterfly. That the vibration is so delicate. . . . You have to make contact with one another to find yourself. It is a wonderful thought that you are able to establish your own identity. You think of that now. By helping other people you are able to stand afar and look at yourself.'

Messages from spirit are true if any number of varied conditions are fulfilled. The 'beauty and fulfilment' of the experience come from recognizing that one's experience is not unique, but can be subsumed under a general symbol.

Frequently the symbol contained in messages takes the form of a brief cameo of particular individuals or activities. A particular type of character is described and the recipient of the message is encouraged to see his own shortcomings in the character traits of the spirit visitor.

To conclude, a general point needs to be made about possession and spirit messages and their relation to insight and control gained over one's internal and external environment. An aspect of this relationship is brought out more clearly by considering the problem of identity in possession.

Theoretically, possession, in contrast to impression, involves the complete taking over of a person's body by another spirit. Hence, all the actions, both verbal and non-verbal, during possession are attributed to the possessing spirit and not to the person possessed. This presents us with a problem. For we cannot say, for example, that Mrs Rhees is Angelique (Mrs Rhees's spirit-guide). This would be a contradiction in terms. On the other hand, spiritualists stress the completeness of successful possession. It is as though Mrs Rhees were keeping an alert watch over her body, whilst at the same time granting complete freedom of movement to the 'right tenant'. The implicit understanding throughout the transactions, however, is that Mrs Rhees is the rightful owner with the power to evict her tenant at a moment's notice should she wish to do so. The arrangements are, in fact, such that both Mrs Rhees and Angelique have a successive share in Mrs Rhees's body.

The spiritualist exegesis of possession suggests an attempt to provide a pictorial representation or explanation of the procedure which will establish its character as one method of social control. Representation of the self as composed of several distinct parts is a common device employed to convey the force of social norms and obligations on the individual. For example, Freud's analysis of psycho-sexual development is consistently seen in terms of the diversification of the self into a number of distinct entities (e.g. Freud, 1930, pp. 62–3 and 73–4).

In large meetings symbols are characterized by their banality. Symbolic objects include numerous bunches of flowers, rays or circles of blue light, rays of blue 'healing' lights, or the reassuring pressure of a friendly hand. These are symbolic objects which are 'given' to members of a spiritualist congregation in the course of a service. In small circles, however, the symbols used assume a much less commonplace and more specifically descriptive nature, whilst at the same time retaining a wide range of applicability. It is widely, though not universally, held that the potency of symbols derives from their unconscious associations. Developing circles aim to discover these associations.

Throughout the exploration of a person's troubles there is a readiness to identify and sympathize. This readiness to share pain and suffering is expressed in the importance attached to physical contact. One of my strongest initial impressions was of the frequency with which spiritualists touch each other. A spiritualist in conversation with another will hold his arm or hand. In the context of a spiritualist service touching is mystically sanctioned and becomes healing. Rubbing and touching have long been recognized as symbols of identification by anthropologists. Evans-Pritchard (1956, pp. 208, 260–2 and 279–81) describes the Nuer as saying: 'I am with you' whilst rubbing another's body.

Interestingly though this sense of solidarity and sympathy is achieved in a context of relative anonymity. There is little interaction between members outside spiritualist circles, since an interest in spiritualism usually provides the only common link between members. Thus spiritualist groups are characterized by their anonymity and their isolation from the rest of the participants' social life. This is in contrast to the character of spirit possession cults in small-scale societies. In such societies relationships have been described as 'multiplex' (Gluckman, 1962, p. 26) in contrast to the 'simplex' relationships of complex societies. This means that the interaction between any two people is 'many-themed' and that the relationship is binding in a number of different ways. Therefore, people who are jointly present when messages are delivered from spirit are subsequently involved in various non-religious activities which are referred to and, hence, affected by communications received during states of spirit possession. In other words, the 'multiplicity' of relationships ensures that what happens within spirit possession cults has an influence on other areas of social life. The situation among Welshtown spiritualists is quite different. Given the anonymity and segregated character of spiritualist groups, what influence can spiritualism have on the secular portion of spiritualist lives? What pressure can spiritualists exert to have the judgments which are mystically sanctioned within meetings, accepted and acted upon outside meetings? In fact, the range of topics considered appropriate for spiritualist meetings is restricted in a way parallel to the restricted sphere of influence which spiritualism is able to exert over areas of life external to it. Spiritualist meetings and messages from spirit are concerned with personal relationships between, for example, husband and wife, or two otherwise closely related kinsfolk. Thus one might suppose that the spiritualist belief system of one partner would influence the other partner to the relationship. However, if messages from spirit were to involve remoter relationships, then they could have little influence over those relationships since agreement in the validity of messages would be lacking.

Thus spiritualism provides an offer of help and support without fear of exposure or the threat of radical changes in a person's life-style. Spiritualism appears sensitive to the fact that alternatives to the traditional feminine role are unclear and, at worst, dangerous. This is hardly surprising in view of the lack of consensus in the literature on feminine roles. The literature on women's liberation is often contradictory and seldom reaches the audience it is aimed at. Beyond personal conviction, there is much confusion and uncertainty about modes of life which eschew the traditional feminine role.

It is significant that a psychoanalyst, albeit a woman, has become sensitive to the high demands on ritualized conformity which the adoption of a traditional feminine role imposes. Hitherto psychoanalysis has epitomized the traditional approach to the role of women. However, Karen Horney, in an essay entitled 'The overvaluation of love' (1968) asks whether what psychoanalysts have hitherto diagnosed as feminine mental health may not, in fact, be a pathological aberration. Horney describes a type of woman whose values all centre on her relationships with men (ibid., p. 185):

These women were as though possessed by a single thought: 'I must have a man'—obsessed with an idea overvalued to the point of absorbing every other thought, so that by comparison all the rest of life seemed stale, flat and unprofitable. The capabilities and interests that most of them possessed either had no meaning at all for them or had lost what meaning they had once had. In other words, conflicts affecting their relations with men were present and could be to a considerable extent relieved, but the actual problem lay not in too little but in too much emphasis on their love life.

Horney's quotation is all the more relevant since, to use a well-known metaphor, Hamlet is referring to 'flesh'. Horney says that the treatment of these women was especially long and arduous because she herself was slow in identifying the problem. It could be said that she was wearing 'diagnostic blinkers'. She says (ibid., p. 186):

> There are two reasons why this problem has only gradually become clarified. On the one hand, the picture presents to a great extent our conception of the truly feminine woman, who has no other aim in life than to lavish devotion upon a man. The second difficulty lies in the analyst himself, who, convinced of the importance of the love life, is consequently disposed to regard the removal of disturbances in this domain as his prime task. He will, therefore, be glad to follow patients who emphasize of their own accord the importance of this sphere into the problem of this kind which they present . . . our discernment quite right and proper in itself, of the importance of heterosexual experience can on occasion blind us to a neurotic overvaluation of and overemphasis of this sphere.

The procedure by which Horney arrives at a diagnosis and distinguishes between healthy traditional femininity and neuroticism is interesting for the light which it sheds on the way in which diagnostic procedures are altered by and reflect changes in social norms relating to feminine behaviour. The point at which the 'discernment of the importance of heterosexual experience' becomes a 'neurotic overvaluation' is determined by current social norms governing feminine behaviour and not by an increasingly sensitive diagnostic procedure which is able to uncover a new pathological condition. Horney, perhaps because she is herself a woman not conforming to norms governing traditional femininity, had readjusted her diagnostic categories in response to a changing social climate. Whereas earlier Freudian analysts regarded any deviation from a traditional feminine role as pathological, Horney regards excessive emphasis on traditional femininity as pathological. Thus the history of psychoanalytic attitudes in this respect is especially interesting in that it reflects both social changes and indicates the ambiguities and difficulties which change engenders.

To conclude, I want to acknowledge the indebtedness and similarity of my treatment of spiritualism with the ideas of Mary Douglas. Her ideas are clearly of relevance. Since this book is concerned with the relationship between ritual and symbolism and social roles and relationships, it falls readily within the scope of Douglas's theoretical field. She says (1970, p. vii): 'The human body is common to us all. Only our social condition varies. The symbols based on the human body are used to express different social experiences.' Thus attitudes which betray a symbolic concern with bodily boundaries reflect a concern with the 'quality of social relations'. For example, a concern with bodily control and the preservation of intact bodily boundaries is a reflection of one's 'experience of a bounded social unit' (ibid.). Conversely, social experience which lacks strong commitment to a group does not make use of 'the essentially bounded character of the human body to express his social concerns' (ibid.). Thus attitudes to bodily control and symbols concerned with bodily control are both regarded as an index both of integration within a group and of the degree of control exercised over the boundaries of the group.

Although my field-work cannot directly support Douglas's hypotheses, it is closely related. For example, spiritualist development implies a particular attitude to bodily control and a particular kind of relationship to the body. This involves both the renunciation of bodily control and a remote vigilance which allows for the immediate resumption of bodily control should this be thought necessary. In so far as spirit medium-ship is practised there is a partial loss of control over bodily boundaries. However, no relationship was found between attitudes of strict bodily control, body symbolism and member-ship of a well-defined group. Ritualization of body image was found to be related to boundaries elsewhere. I have already suggested a relationship between a ritualized body-image and the acceptance of a traditionally feminine role. Structurally the most significant feature of a traditionally feminine role is its separation from the masculine social role. Thus boundaries are drawn between the acknowledged spheres of male and female work, social activities, interests and emotional orienta-tions. In short, male and female life-styles are so different that men and women are thought to inhabit two different worlds. Whether this kind of boundary related to role segregation is one which can legitimately be said to give rise to the ex-perience of a bounded social unit is doubtful. Explanations in terms of boundaries can become dangerous. For, it is a logical truth relevant to many worlds that they are individuated both in terms of what they are and in terms of what they are not. In other words, in terms of 'inside' and 'outside'. Thus of necessity if we stop to consider any social phenomenon for long enough, or carefully enough, we shall find that it involves boundaries. However, we have discovered a logical truth about the structure of our experience and not an empirical truth about the world. This does not mean that I find explanations which relate bodily boundaries to social boundaries useless. The universal presence of boundaries should merely make us cautious in assessing their explanatory value.

Chapter 7   Religious and therapeutic encounters

Welsh spiritualist activities have been described in earlier chapters. Certain more theoretical questions remain to be answered in this concluding chapter.

Throughout it has been implied that spiritualist meetings have a strong psychotherapeutic element. However, such an implication, if left unexamined, raises more questions than it can claim to answer. The term 'psychotherapy' is a notoriously difficult one and like that of 'mental health' it occupies the borderland between several disciplines. In claiming that spiritualist meetings offer therapeutic benefits it becomes necessary to examine such terms more precisely. A theoretical framework which embraces both religions and therapeutic encounters is needed.

One of the best definitions of psychotherapy, found in a standard textbook on clinical psychology, expresses my own reservations and illustrates the initial difficulties raised by an attempted comparison of psychotherapeutic procedures: 'Psychotherapy is an unidentified technique applied to unspecified problems with unpredictable outcomes. . . . For this technique we recommend rigorous training' (Raimy, 1950). In a more careful tone Jonathan Glover (1971) asks where eccentricity shades into mental illness. He considers the question with reference to the eccentric behaviour of Squire Mytton of Shrewsbury described by both Virginia Woolf (1932) and Edith Sitwell (1970). According to Glover, Mytton's behaviour is merely exuberant and unconventional until the element of harm or self-injury enters. When, however, the squire allows several thousand pounds to be blown away through the window of his carriage, or, after a particularly satisfying dinner, tries to 'chase away' a hiccough by setting fire to his night-shirt, then, Glover argues, the concept of mental illness is appropriate. If we accept Glover's definition of mental illness as corresponding in some measure to current, common-sense ideas on the subject, then, by implication psychotherapy is concerned with the alleviation of suffering. However, although according to this definition suffering is a necessary condition of mental illness it is not, of course, a sufficient condition.

Moreover, if religion is concerned with suffering, then it can be argued that all religions have a psychotherapeutic element. Frank (1961) adopts this broad comparative approach. He examines religious revivalism, thought reform and psychotherapy in terms of their attempts to provide the individual with a more successful 'assumptive world', a belief system which makes better sense of the universe and the believer's role in it. Similarly Kiev in his article (1964) on the psychotherapeutic aspects of Pentecostal sects claims to be interested in the 'mental health potentialities' of religious behaviour. Oates (1955) describes the religious way of life as 'a therapeutic aid'.

Whilst such comparisons are appropriate they do not take one far. Both elements of comparison are left undefined. To attribute an unknown benefit, namely therapy, to religion is to say little about the processes involved in ritual healing or exploration. A possible framework within which to examine both religious and therapeutic activities is based on Aberle's classification (1966) of social movements in terms of the location of problems and difficulties and the ascription of responsibility. Aberle is concerned with the classification of social movements and he offers certain dimensions in terms of which this can be achieved. 'One is the dimension of the locus of change sought. The other is the dimension of the amount of change sought. As to locus, a movement may aim to change individuals or some supra-individual system—the economic order, the technological order, the political order, the law, a total society or culture, the world or indeed the cosmos. As to amount of change, movements may aim at total or partial change' (ibid., p. 316). On the basis of these two dimensions, he provides a classification consisting of four distinct types of social movements which he represents as follows:

Classification of Social Movements

		Locus of change	
		Supra-individual	Individual
Amount of change	Total	Transformative	Redemptive
	Partial	Reformative	Alterative

The four possibilities identified are, of course, pure types and any actual social movement may contain elements of each type. Aberle discusses the 'constant characteristics' of transformative and redemptive movements. Whether a movement assumes a transformative or redemptive character will depend upon the degree of felt 'relative deprivation'. The greater the experience of deprivation the more sweeping the felt need for changes.

The details of Aberle's typology need not be considered but the relevance to the present discussion is obvious. Both psychiatric treatments and religious practice can be subsumed under one of the four categories which Aberle's typology provides. They can be examined in terms of the locus and extent of the changes which they seek. This single-minded approach avoids some of the difficulties otherwise encountered in a comparative endeavour which aims to order disparate interpretations. Such a framework encourages the perception of social configurations associated with a particular ascription of responsibility for difficulties.

Thus the appropriate question to ask in the case of psychiatry is whether the individual or his social environment is felt to be the source of difficulties. Similarly, with religious commitment one can establish whether this involves feelings of inadequacy attributed to the believer or to society at large. To simplify, the traditional medical model of psychiatric illness speaks in terms of individual vulnerabilities, thus locating the problem within the individual. The family interaction model, on the other hand, sees difficulties as resulting from inadequacies in family communication which, taken to their logical conclusion, reflect the inadequacies of society at large.

Similarly, all religions hold out the promise of better methods of dealing with difficulties, of more efficient coping techniques. However, some religions locate problems in the individual lifestyle, others locate problems in the shortcomings of the world. In the former case the individual does not come up to society's standards; in the latter case society does not come up to the individual's standards. For example, among Pentecostal sects confession and a review of the individual's past history and sins are essential ingredients of conversion. Among spiritualist groups, on the other hand, emphasis is much more on understanding and coming to terms with the shortcomings of the 'outside' world.

Reflecting these differences in the distribution of difficulties and the attribution of responsibility are differences in religious and therapeutic activity and technique. Where difficulties are held to lie within the individual changes have to be wrought within him. This can be done either by physical treatment or by providing new insights or guides for living as in the case of psychoanalysis and the Pentecostal sects. In fact the similarities between certain ecstatic conversion experiences and certain forms of drug therapy in terms of their physiological effects have been noticed (Sargent, 1957).

This theoretical framework is one simplified way of exploring the differences between Protestantism and Catholicism. These two religions exert different types of control over the individual. Moreover, the two religions also conceptualize the source of difficulties and suffering in different ways. Weber says (1948, p. 280): ' "From what" and "for what" one wished to be redeemed and, let us not forget, "could be" redeemed, depended upon one's image of the world'. The Protestant and the Catholic answer to the question of what religion is saving one from are very different from one another. Catholicism saves the individual from sins and the areligious self. Protestantism saves the individual from the corruption of society by providing an alternative rigid model of social behaviour. In each case the rewards are different. Catholicism offers paradise. Protestantism is transformative and offers a better life on earth.

Where problems are seen to stem from the social milieu of the individual the emphasis is on creating a new social and spiritual environment. Spiritualist circles provide one example of an attempt to provide a more worthwhile society. Therapeutic communities and therapeutic groups provide examples from the psychiatric field. To the extent that a taxonomy of religious and therapeutic involvement can be constructed along the lines suggested, then spiritualist groups belong to a category which includes certain therapeutic groups and communities.

Another useful theoretical appraisal of religious commitment and one which can most readily be transferred to the field of psychiatry is that provided by Glock and Stark (1965). The authors introduce their subject by examining the dimensions of religious commitment. If 'religiosity' is being assessed then it is important to know which dimension is being used. A religion may be high on some dimensions and low on others. In fact, dimensions may be mutually exclusive. The possible dimensions or indicators for measuring religious commitment which Glock and Stark list are as follows:

Religious belief (ideological dimension)
Religious practice (ritual dimension)
Religious feeling (experiential dimension)
Religious knowledge (intellectual dimension)
Religious effects (consequential dimension)

These dimensions are used as indicators of religious commitment. However, they are equally applicable in assessing therapeutic commitment. Different dimensions are held to be important by different religions and different forms of psychiatric treatment. Early Methodism laid great stress on the consequential dimension of religious commitment as do physical forms of psychiatric treatment. Spiritualism and psychoanalysis, on the other hand, lay great stress on the experiential dimension—on personal knowledge and insight— with less importance attached to the effects of religious and therapeutic involvement. For example, it is more important to know why one steals than to stop stealing.

Glock and Stark also suggest ways of classifying religion and therapeutic experience by formulating a taxonomy of religious experience. They suggest that the relationship between the believer and the divine be conceptualized as a social encounter. Such a conceptualization leads to four possible types of configuration of inter-actor relations.

(a) The human actor simply notes the presence of the divine actor. This is described as the confirming experience.

(b) The mutual presence of the two actors is acknowledged. This is described as the responsive experience.

(c) The awareness of mutual presence is replaced by an affective relationship. This is termed the ecstatic experience.

(d) The human actor perceives himself as a confidant or a fellow participant in action with the divine actor. This is termed the revelational experience. The types of relationship are placed in order of frequency of occurrence and thus follow the pattern of more general social experience. That is, one is usually, though not necessarily, an acquaintance before one becomes a friend and a friend before one becomes a lover.

If 'therapist' is substituted for 'divine actor', this taxonomy can be applied to the field of therapy in order to identify similarities and dissimilarities between religions and psychiatric practice. Spiritualist groups come in the last category, as do certain forms of group therapy.

This view of society as being potentially good and possessed of healing powers is not unique. Field-work material has provided anthropologists with an opportunity to compare the distribution of ideas of good and evil as between man, society and nature. For example, a frequent constellation of values attributes innate goodness to man and nature and powers of evil and corruption to society. Contrasting with this set of values is a belief in the inherent badness of man and nature in so far as these fall outside the influence of society together with a trust in the beneficial effects of social life. These two sets of attitudes provide the *a priori* and unquestioned starting point of the seventeenth-century political philosophers. Rousseau saw society as corrupting and man and nature as good. Hobbes saw man and nature as destructive and society as exercising a tempering influence.

So far I have indicated in a general way the similarity between psychotherapeutic groups and spiritualist circles in terms of the healing properties which each is thought to possess. It now remains to examine in more detail some of the structural features of therapy in groups which emphasize their similarities with the activities of spiritualist circles.

Henry Walton describes the therapeutic process as follows: 'The basis of group therapy is the interactive network among members rather than what each individual independently "as a person" brings to the group. Indeed, "here and now" material, the action actually taking place in a session which all members witness and contribute to is more useful than descriptions of early experiences during the childhood of a particular patient' (1971, p. 24). In other words, group meetings are important because of the interaction which takes place between members. 'What the patient displays during the sessions is his range of habitual solutions to the conflicts he evokes in his personal relationships' (ibid., p. 34). Problems, solutions to problems and ideals are assessed by group standards and either classified as 'real' or 'unreal'. 'The patient in this way is expected in the group not only to reveal his assumptive world, but to try out new behaviours, and then to transfer them to his life outside the group in a way that improves his social

effectiveness' (ibid.). Thus, 'group analytic groups' are a deliberate attempt to construct a definite, bounded social unit within which a model of social interaction can be provided. But in
spiritualist circles, the therapeutic analogues are a natural
and unselfconscious outgrowth of ritual and healing activities
and beliefs rather than being the result of deliberate planning.

At the level of physical description a number of further
similarities emerge. Like spiritualist circles therapeutic groups
can either be 'open' or 'closed'. The most frequent type of
therapeutic group is the 'slow-open' variety. In such groups
a new member is introduced when an old member leaves,
vacancies sometimes being advertised in weekly journals. Thus,
theoretically a group can continue to exist indefinitely even
though it may have acquired an entirely new membership.
There is, however, an emphasis on group structure. Thus an
absentee from the group is represented by an empty chair.
Group membership should consist of between five and ten
people and should include both males and females. A group is
led by one or two therapists. Importance is attached to the
regularity of meetings with regard to both time and place.
Interaction or 'pairing' outside the group is discouraged.
During sessions chairs are grouped in a circle so that each
member is totally visible to every other member. This emphasis
on total visibility perhaps comes from the fact that 'tension
leakage' occurs in the hands or the feet (Ekman and Friesen,
1969). Facial expression of feeling is more readily controlled
than is bodily expression which can provide 'deception clues'.
Finally, discussion is not task-oriented but 'free-floating'.

These features of therapeutic groups are equally features of
spiritualist circles. Both kinds of group aim to provide a model
of social interaction which members of the group aim to
imitate in their life outside the group.

Comparisons can also be made between spiritualist circles
and other types of therapeutic group, namely, 'therapeutic
communities'.[1] The healing properties of the community and

---

[1] The first therapeutic community was established by Maxwell Jones at
Belmont after the Second World War as a rehabilitation centre for soldiers

of interaction within it have been precisely identified in terms of a number of organizational principles. There is general agreement between writers on the therapeutic community as to what these principles are (Jones, 1968; Clark, 1964; Rapoport, 1960). Rapoport lists the following features as necessary ingredients of a therapeutic community (ibid., 54):

1 Democratization   3 Communalism
2 Permissiveness   4 Reality confrontation

Democratization refers to equal participation in decision-making procedures. Permissiveness refers to the desirability of uncensored expression of thought and feeling. Communalism refers to the interchangeability and lack of specialization of roles within the community. Reality confrontation refers to acceptance of an interpersonal, but intra-community, interpretation of the world. However, the most striking characteristic of the category of groups which embraces both spiritualist circles and therapeutic communities is the idea that a total society may possess healing properties. Rapoport (1960, p. 10) expresses the idea as follows:

> According to this approach, the hospital is not seen as a
> place where patients are classified and stored, nor a place
> where one group of individuals (the medical staff) gives
> treatment to another group of individuals (the patients)
> according to the model of general medical hospitals;
> but as a place which is organized as a community in
> which everyone is expected to make some contribution
> towards the shared goals of creating a social organization
> that will have healing properties.

In other words, everyone contributes and everyone receives benefits. The comparison of spiritualist groups and therapeutic

suffering from 'shell-shock'. Since that time, although few other such centres have, in fact, been established, the idea of the therapeutic community has been much discussed and has gained popularity. The original community set up by Maxwell Jones now functions largely as a treatment centre for adolescents and young adults with problems of anti-social behaviour. The community has been renamed the Henderson Community and its inmates have been labelled 'sociopaths'.

communities can, of course, only be sustained at one level, since spiritualist groups are manifestly *not* communities.

The overt similarities between the organizational principles of therapeutic communities and spiritualist circles are striking. The four key principles underlying the idea of a therapeutic community are equally central to spiritualist belief and practice. However, the same principles are expressed in religious language. For example, much emphasis is placed on the equality of all spiritualists in terms of the possession of mediumistic powers at least in a latent form. Similarly, there is an emphasis on submission to spirit, in the sense of taking on whatever conditions are imposed by spirit or giving out whatever messages are received from spirit. In line with the equality of all, members are not differentiated by being assigned different tasks within the group. Finally, there are pressures to accept a group formulated view of 'reality'. Such pressures exist in all groups but they are especially strong in a group which sees its main task as one of receiving the truth from spirit, or of defining ultimate reality.

Within the spiritualist context I have already alluded to the strain and conflict inherent in the juxtaposition of these principles. The belief in the equality of all circle members is one which in practice produces considerable conflict between mediums and groups competing for spiritual recognition. The positive value attached to the absence of censorship, the injunction to would-be mediums to 'give it out as it is given', nevertheless produces strain when actually implemented. The conflicting views with respect to the moral implications of uninhibited expression of spirit communication have already been described. Similar conflicts can be identified within a therapeutic community. Some of these have been described by Rapoport (1960). For example, although theoretically power is said to be equally distributed among the members of the community, situations of crisis and conflict reveal its real if unacknowledged locus. In such situations submerged social roles re-emerge.

A further difficulty shared by both spiritualist groups and

therapeutic communities and stemming from similarities in their structure, related to the processes whereby community definitions of reality are achieved. How is a final definition of a problematic situation and its relevant context formulated? Within the spiritualist circle difficulties arise because each member is thought to have equal access to spirit and, hence, conflicting interpretations of messages from spirit may arise. The defining process is rendered as complex where the entire therapeutic community consisting of up to a hundred members is involved. How in this instance is universal agreement reached? The process whereby such consensus is established bears an uncanny and unflattering resemblance to the process whereby Rousseau's general will is discovered. Given this lack of specificity as regards authoritative defining procedures the scope for conflict and manipulation is vast.

Many other religious groups and therapeutic groups could be compared and contrasted. However, the purposes of this chapter are merely to indicate the possibility and usefulness of a particular approach or theoretical framework. Its wider application remains to be tried.

So far comparisons have drawn out the similarities between spiritualist circles and group analytic groups and therapeutic communities. However, it is also necessary to provide contrasts. The Scientology movement provides a different interpretation of the source of problems and, following on from this, different methods of dealing with problems. Scientologist doctrine involves an ascent through a succession of hierarchically organized stages of insight and understanding, until one reaches the state of being 'clear'. The term itself is evocative. To an anthropologist it has definite associations with the institution of poison ordeals among certain Central African tribes. Among the Lele, for example, when a person is accused of practising witchcraft, one way of demonstrating his good faith and re-instating his forfeited dignity is by drinking a special poison (Douglas, 1963). If he survives then his name is cleared and he is purged of guilt and blame. Similarly, if the Scientologist neophyte survives the lengthy and expensive process of attaining the state of 'clear', then he is purged of any stigma attaching to the previous mismanagement of problems. In this way Scientology seems to present itself as a form of therapy by offering a labelling device of its own for countering the established labelling processes in society at large. The original problems are held to stem from within the individual and there are clearly defined stages for overcoming these problems. The Scientologist is never part of a group, but each level of development involves participation in a dyadic relationship with a Scientologist occupying a superior position in the hierarchical structure. Scientologists have encountered considerable problems over the question of whether Scientology is a religion or a form of therapy. The latest consensus of opinion among Scientologists is that it is a philosophy and a religion but not a form of therapy. However, such distinctions are in some measure arbitrary since all religions have some therapeutic elements, just as most forms of therapy acquire some ritualistic elements.

So far the theme of this chapter has been concerned with comparing religious with psychotherapeutic activity. However, there are dangers in this approach which need to be identified. All religions offer tools for handling life's problems and suffering, but it has been suggested that some religions are better equipped for handling problems than others. That is, that they are psychotherapeutic in the sense of dealing with or 'containing psychiatric illness'. The implication is that some, if not all, forms of religious preoccupation are a defence against 'madness'. The description of church membership as facilitating 'mature religious experience' (Carnier, 1965, p. 285) and by implication the assessment of sect membership as an expression of 'spiritual immaturity', provides an example of this outlook. Similar views can be found among a number of other writers. Roger Bastide (1972, p. 137), for example, writes: 'The sects are closed communities protecting their members against mental disorder.' Oates (1955) describes Baptist missionaries in the southern states of America as being shielded from 'psychosis' by a religious way of life. Catton (1957) describes a 'sectarian tendency' produced by profound feelings of psychological inadequacy and frustration.

The problem which now emerges is of the need to open up the possibilities of exploring the therapeutic elements in religion without leaving the door wide open for the view which claims that sect membership is a functional alternative to, or protection against, ultimate psychiatric breakdown. There is a danger of labelling religion as mature or immature according to how much healing or therapy it provides. This approach introduces the two notions of spiritual and emotional immaturity and merges both in the notion of the sectarian personality. However, the appraisal of religious commitment in terms of its mental health advantages is one which produces discomfort for the believer as well as the sociologist. It makes tacit use of a division of society into the healthy and unhealthy. The need for such a division requires explanation by the sociologist, rather than unquestioning acceptance. It is restatement of the dichotomy between the religion of the sick and the healthy soul first introduced by William James (1960). These two religions differ according to the importance and emphasis which they assign to evil and suffering. James (ibid., p. 168) summarizes the difference as follows:

> we can see how great an antagonism may naturally arise between the healthy-minded way of viewing life and the way that takes all this experience of evil as something essential. To this latter way, the morbid-minded way, as we might call it, healthy-mindedness pure and simple seems unspeakably blind and shallow. To the healthy-minded way, on the other hand, the way of the sick soul seems unmanly and diseased. With their grubbing in rat holes instead of living in the light; with their manufacture of fears and preoccupation with every unwholesome kind of misery, there is something almost

obscene about these children of wrath and cravers of second birth.

The irreconcilability of the religions of health and of sickness is explained by reference to the sickness or health of the soul, the sick soul being the Jamesian equivalent of the sectarian personality. However, this explanation is insufficient, since it uses as explanation that which needs to be explained, namely, sickness. To the extent that sickness is introduced in the spiritualist context it has been treated as 'sociosomatic'. That is, it is seen as a means of mirroring difficulties in social roles and relationships. Thus both the experience of disability and the form which religious involvement takes are related to features of the social experience of believers. Illness, as the language in which interest in spiritualist activities is expressed, and possession experiences involving illness within circles are both related to difficulties connected with a traditional feminine role. It may well be the case that the so-called religion of the sick soul is beyond the understanding of so-called healthy-minded religion, but this may be not because of any intrinsic morbidness of mind of its believers. It may simply be that the social experiences and biographies of each are remote from one another. Since religion, like art, is a mirror to life it gives different emphasis to suffering and pain.

Bibliography

Chapter 1
Caplan, Gerald (1972), 'Support systems', unpublished paper.
Lewis, Ioan (1966), 'Spirit possession and deprivation cults', *Man*, N.S. 1(3), 307–29.
Parsons, Talcott (1950), *The Social System*, Chicago: Free Press.
Petitpierre, Dom Robert (Ed.) (1972), *Exorcism*, London: S.P.C.K.
Young, Jock (1971), *The Drugtakers*, London: Paladin.

Chapter 2
Horton, Robin (1969), 'Spirit possession among the Kalabari', in Beattie, J. and Middleton, J. (eds), *Spirit Mediumship and Society in Africa*, London: Routledge & Kegan Paul.

Chapter 3
Balint, Michael (1964), *The Doctor, the Patient and the Illness*, London: Tavistock.
Bentham, Jeremy (1789), *An Introduction to the Principles of Morals and Legislation*, Edited by J. H. Burns and H. L. A. Hart (1970), London University Press.
Bradley, Francis Herbert (1888), 'On Pleasure, Pain, Desire and Volition', *Mind*, xiii, 2.
Douglas, Mary (1970), *Natural Symbols*, London: Barrie & Rockliff.
Fortes, Meyer (1959), *Oedipus and Job in a West African Religion*, Cambridge University Press.
Koos, Earl (1954), *The Health of Regionville: What the People Thought and Did about It*, Connecticut: Hafner.
Laing, Ronald (1971), *The Self and Others*, Harmondsworth: Penguin.
Middleton, John (1960), *Lugbara Religion*, Oxford University Press.
Robinson, David (1971), *The Process of Becoming Ill*, London: Routledge & Kegan Paul.

Ryle, Gilbert (1949), *The Concept of Mind*, London: Hutchinson.
Skultans, Vieda (1970), 'The symbolic significance of menstruation and the menopause', *Man*, n.s. 5, 639–51.
Tambiah, S. (1970), *Buddhism and the Spirit Cults in North East Thailand*, Cambridge University Press.
Wittgenstein, Ludwig (1963), *The Philosophical Investigations*, Oxford: Basil Blackwell.
Zola, Irving (1966), 'Culture and symptoms: an analysis of patients' presenting complaints', *American Sociological Review*, 31, 615–29.
Zborowski, Mark (1952), 'Cultural components in responses to pain', *Journal of Social Issues*, 4, 16–30.

Chapter 4

Bradley, Francis Herbert (1930), *Aphorisms*, Oxford: Clarendon Press.
Gluckman, Max (1956), *Custom and Conflict*, Oxford: Basil Blackwell.
Harris, Grace (1957), 'Possession "hysteria" in a Kenya tribe', *American Anthropologist*, 61, 1046–66.
Horton, Robin (1969), 'Spirit possession among the Kalabari', in Beattie, J. and Middleton, J. (eds), *Spirit Mediumship and Society in Africa*, London: Routledge & Kegan Paul.
Lewis, Ioan (1966), 'Spirit possession and deprivation cults', *Man*, n.s. 1(3), 307–29.
Messing, Simon (1958), 'Group therapy and social status in the Zar cult of Ethiopia', *American Anthropologist*, 60 (6), 1120–6.
Mischel, Walter and Mischel, Frances (1958), 'Psychological aspects of spirit possession', *American Anthropologist*, 60, 249–60.

Chapter 5

Glock, Charles and Stark, Rodney (1965), *Religion and Society in Tension*, Chicago: Rand McNally.
Hollander, Marc (1964), *Leaders, Groups and Influence*, New York: Oxford University Press.
Lacey, Colin (1970), *Hightown Grammar: the School as a Social System*, Manchester University Press.

Chapter 6

Berger, John (1967), *A Fortunate Man*, London: Allen Lane, The Penguin Press.
Douglas, Mary (1970), *Natural Symbols*, London: Barrie & Rockliff.

Evans-Pritchard, E. E. (1956), *Nuer Religion*, Oxford: Clarendon Press.

Field, M. G. (1960), *The Search for Security*, London: Faber.

Freud, Sigmund (1930), *Civilization and its Discontents*, London: Hogarth Press.

Gluckman, Max (ed.) (1962), *Essays on the Ritual of Social Relations*, Manchester University Press.

Horney, Karen (1968), 'The overvaluation of love', in *Feminine Psychology*, London: Routledge & Kegan Paul.

Ucko, L. E. (1967), 'Early stress experiences mirrored in "world" play tests at five years', *Human Development*, 10 (2), 107–27.

Chapter 7

Aberle, David (1966), *The Peyote Religion among the Navaho*, Chicago: Aldine.

Bastide, Roger (1972), *The Sociology of Mental Disorder*, London: Routledge & Kegan Paul.

Carnier, Hervé (1965), *The Sociology of Religious Belonging*, London: Routledge & Kegan Paul.

Catton, W. R. (1957), 'What kind of people does a religious cult attract?', *American Sociological Review*, 22, 561–6.

Clark, David (1964), *Administrative Therapy: the Role of the Doctor in the Therapeutic Community*, London: Tavistock.

Douglas, Mary (1963), *The Lele of the Kasai*, Oxford University Press.

Ekman, P. and Friesen, W. V. (1969), 'The repertoire of non-verbal behaviour categories, origins, usages and coding', *Semiotica* 1, 49–98.

Frank, J. D. (1961), *Healing and Persuasion: A Comparative Study of Psychotherapy*, London: Oxford University Press.

Glock, Charles and Stark, Rodney (1965), *Religion and Society in Tension*, Chicago: Rand McNally.

Glover, Jonathan (1971), *Responsibility*, London: Routledge & Kegan Paul.

James, William (1960), *The Varieties of Religious Experience*, London: Fontana.

Jones, Maxwell (1968), *Social Psychiatry in Practice*, Harmondsworth: Penguin.

Kiev, Ari (1964), 'Psychotherapeutic aspects of Pentecostal sects among West Indian Immigrants to England', *British Journal of Sociology*, 15, 129–38.

Oates, Wayne E. (1955), *Religious Factors in Mental Illness*, London: Allen & Unwin.

Raimy, V. (1950), *Training in Clinical Psychology*, New York: Prentice-Hall.

Rapoport, Robert (1960), *Community as Doctor*, London: Social Science Paperbacks.

Sargent, William R. (1957), *Battle for the Mind*, London: Heinemann.

Sitwell, Edith (1970), *English Eccentrics*, Harmondsworth: Penguin.

Walton, Henry (ed.) (1971), *Small Group Psychotherapy*, Harmondsworth: Penguin.

Weber, Max (1948), *From Max Weber: Essays in Sociology*, eds H. H. Gerth and C. Wright Mills, London: Routledge & Kegan Paul.

Woolf, Virginia (1932), *The Common Reader* (2nd series), London: Hogarth Press, pp. 126–31.

Index